Pop Fic Review

Pop Fic Review

a literary anthology that embraces and challenges
the idea of popular fiction

Edited by
Hannah Strom-Martin and Erin Underwood

UNDERWORDS
Marblehead, Massachusetts

UNDERWORDS
48 Hawkes Street
Marblehead, MA 01945
www.underwordsblog.com

ISBN 13: 978-0-615-54382-6

Printed in the United States of America
by CreateSpace.

First Edition: 2011
10 9 8 7 6 5 4 3 2 1

Dedicated to Tom and Tony.

With special thanks to the Stonecoast MFA community,
our mentors, friends, and families
who helped to make this anthology possible.

Contents

Introduction

Hannah Strom-Martin and Erin Underwood

What is "pop fic"? That's the question that's haunted us as we've assembled the anthology you're holding in your hands. "Fiction" is easy (encompassing everything from Harold Bloom to Snooki), but "popular" is treacherous—reminiscent of Warhol's soup cans. One man's "popular" is another man's faded rock star.

Those of us who regularly commit popular fictions recognize them when we see them. They're the weird (yet cool) kids on the block, wearing concert T-shirts and a touch of noir. They're those crazy flights where you board in Selma, Indiana and end up in Neverland. Often they're infused with speculative elements (you're going to find some of those in here), but in a world increasingly concerned with entertaining itself, they might also be Jeff Kass's "Orbs," which has a few things to say about games of all kinds, or Julie L. Martin's remembrances of the '80s, or Patricia Smith's poem, "Hauling Them Home" (whose imagery, evoking a gritty noir-like voice that speaks to the daily struggle of the masses, is certainly *at home* here). "Pop" may also mean "pop culture"—the headlines, fine arts, and urban legends that infuse modern literature in all its forms. Those entries in the *Pop Fic Review* that aren't technically fiction still connect deeply to popular culture, tapping into influences both historical and current.

The *Pop Fic Review*, then, is an anthology featuring multiple literary forms that all in some way embrace the concept of popular fiction. It has one other common denominator. Each piece you find here was written by a member of the Stonecoast MFA community.

Stonecoast is a competitive MFA program in creative writing hosted by the University of Southern Maine—and a place where mixing genres and forms is not only accepted, but encouraged. Unique among MFA programs, Stonecoast even has a "Pop-Fiction" track, allowing those of us as obsessed with Tolkien as with Tolstoy to earn a terminal degree in creative writing.

Contributors to this anthology include current Stonecoast students, alumni, and faculty from all concentrations within the program. Comprising pieces from fiction writers, essayists, memoirists, and poets, the *Pop Fic Review* confronts the definition of "pop" through the literature of contributors who have come up with their own unique expressions of what "Pop Fic" embodies.

Which is a fancy way of saying that pop may be an SOS written on the back of a zombie.

Or a siren with a recording contract.

Or a bouquet of hand-painted fans plummeting from the apex of an ornamental bridge into waters patrolled by djinn in realms presided over by matriarchal artisans.

We're glad we could clear that up for you.

That sound you hear is your literary expectations going pop.

Painting the Air
James Patrick Kelly

"I'm sick of dusting her fans!" Jaya stepped out of her pants and tossed them at Hool, her djinn lover. They fluttered across the room and spun to rest under his bed. "Grinding pigment for that old crow's paint. Lugging bolts of silk from the market." She unstrung the laces of her shirt and let it fall from her shoulders. The damp, smoky air of the room seemed to cling to her skin. It was a relief to be naked.

"Apprentice work," agreed Hool. "It's beneath you." He was one of several dozen djinn exiled to the Happy City to do penance for sins he claimed no mortal could ever understand. He was presenting tonight as a snake-man; the nubs at the ends of his vestigial arms and legs wriggled bonelessly. "I can't believe your parents signed a four-year contract."

"Feels more like forty." Jaya had long since decided that it was time to put down the broom and pick up her brushes. Of course, she was allowed an hour in the evening to sketch Mahir's masterpieces on cheap fans of paper and bamboo. And yes, the guild of fan makers permitted Jaya to sell those crude copies in the market. But Jaya was eager to paint lilies and herons and the learned ladies of the castle. On silk, in a studio of her own.

After all, Jaya was twenty-two years old and an artist. Not a servant.

"I think she's trying to make me quit." Jaya threaded her fingers into her long hair and lifted it off her shoulders. Her neck felt hot. "Sometimes I hate her."

"She's afraid of what you'll do on your own."

"I want my release." She let the hair fall. "That's all I really want, Hool. Just that."

"Too small a wish." Hool coiled up her arm. "You have to think bigger."

Jaya sighed. She shared his bed in part because she hoped he might grant her the true wish, which would end his exile. But the heart of a djinn was a mystery. If they had hearts.

He pulled her to him. "Come lie with me, and I'll kick all four of those years under the blanket." He flicked his forked tongue at her. "There's no room in my bed for worry or regret."

She settled next to him and brushed the back of her forefinger against his long spine "Not smooth tonight, Hool," she said. "Rough." Sometimes his dry scales tickled across her belly and spoiled the mood. "Big. And hairy."

Hool sighed and passed her the censer. "Ape?" he said. "Bear?"

Jaya stuck her face close to the smoldering feather in the censer and breathed deeply. "Surprise me." The honeyed smoke curled into her nose and stretched her lungs.

"Porcupine?"

"It's pleasure I'm wishing for just now, djinn." It was a joke: she knew he wasn't going to make anyone's wish come true that night. When Jaya giggled, smoke leaked from the corner of her mouth. "Pain for some other time."

"A moment, then." Hool's flesh surged and turned cloudy. The skin around his head split apart as he began to molt. As his smooth body slithered from the sheath of scales, shoulders and hips formed and limbs unfolded. Down sprouted into a stubble of hair and blunt claws curled from toe pads. The fur was gray with rust highlights on the back and buff on the belly and legs. The canines glistened in the lamplight; the tongue that rolled between them was the color of raw steak. The wolf arched, ears back, hindquarters lowered in submission.

"Here," he growled, "you are the master." He burrowed his snout between her legs.

Jaya offered the master her palette but Mahir paid no attention. She squatted beneath the easel and held a sensing brush up to the leaf of her utmost fan, the one she was entering in the Festival. The handle of the brush was bound to her right wrist, palm, and forefinger with silk ribbons. Mahir had the tremors and Jaya could tell that this was not one of her good days. The only way the master could do finish work was with the brushes that read her thoughts. The Festival of the Fans was already underway; the competition was but three days away and she had yet to fold the leaf of her fan or mount it on its ivory slips.

"Yi-yi!" Mahir straightened painfully, stumped around the easel twice and then stopped to the left of it, considering her work. Jaya watched her with a mixture of envy and disgust. The master insisted that performance was as necessary as draftsmanship to find the spirit of her subject: she spent as much time posturing and yipping as she did putting paint on silk. In her youth, crowds would gather to watch her work, as much entranced by her showmanship as her artistry. But when the fickle onlookers began to visit the studios of the other master fan makers in the Happy City, Mahir had closed her doors. Now only Jaya witnessed her antics.

Mahir had been trying to finish the wings of a dragonfly for the past two weeks, her thin brush darting to limn an indigo filigree of veins across the cyan wash of the membrane. She had used a cool palette to fill her lines: a pale, viridian fringe of cattail with emerald highlights edged a dark pond, a gray-green willow branch reached down from above. Jaya admired the composition—although she would have included a stronger horizontal—but she had no use for the subject.

"A muchness of color. The thin needs to be darker," Mahir said. "Charcoal, quick." She inclined her head toward the shelf of pigments. "Quick now, you silly girl."

Jaya sprang from her stool and pinched black powder from its jar. She rubbed thumb and forefinger together over the thick indigo smudge on the palette and charcoal wisped down.

"Again," said Mahir. "But softer, soft."

Jaya had just begun to sprinkle more of the dust when Mahir slapped her hand away. "Good, that's good." The master snatched the palette from her.

Jaya wiped her fingers on her apron and sat. She was trying not to pout, but it was hard. "Patri is painting the High Constable Herself's castle on her utmost fan," she said.

There was no sound in the studio but the click of the brush against the palette.

"And a rosebush," said Jaya. "Red roses."

Mahir pressed her head hard against her shoulder to see the fan leaf better and then held her shaking hand close to the easel. "Red is for butchers and hat-makers and clowns," she murmured. "It shouts."

"It shouts I will take the prize."

"Color doesn't touch the spirit of things." Mahir's lips pressed tight and she glared at the dragonfly on her utmost fan. Then despite her trembling, the sensing brush held steady and Mahir struck a perfect line on the wing. "And red usually hides a truth." She grunted in satisfaction and stepped back to admire what she had done.

Jaya thought the sensing brush was a cheat. She had already decided she would never use one, no matter how old she got. "You're dripping again."

Mahir jerked as if she had been stung; a drop of dark indigo splattered on the floor. She had always prided herself on neatness and restraint. "So." She aimed the brush at Jaya. "You have seen this fan?"

"Everybody has." Jaya wasn't going to let Mahir make her feel guilty about scouting her rival. "There's a line out the front of her studio watching her paint it." A master ought to know the fashion, so she could put it aside.

"This is about politics, Jaya, not about fans. Next she'll be painting the High Constable Herself's ugly face on her utmost."

"She wants the prize."

Mahir's grin was all bumps and wrinkles. "And you?"

"I'm just an apprentice," said Jaya.

"You seethe with ambition, apprentice."

"To make fans of my own? Yes."

Mahir pulled a stool up to the easel and stepped onto it. She swayed for a moment and Jaya bolted upright and braced herself to catch the master if she fell. Mahir waved her away.

"I want to leave, Master," said Jaya. "Give me your blessing."

Mahir placed her hands to either side of her head, framing her view of the leaf of the utmost fan. "You're not ready."

Jaya watched indigo paint dribbling down the handle of the sensing brush strapped to the master's hand. "You mean you're not ready."

Mahir let her hands fall to her side. "I wonder what you've learned here, Jaya." For a moment the master fan maker stood high on the stool, as if posing for a statue that no one would ever think to carve. She surveyed her cluttered studio and her collection of utmosts, twelve of which had won the High Constable Herself's prize at the Festival of the Fans. Then she dismissed them with a stroke of her brush. "Sometimes," she said, "I think I might as well be painting the air."

Hool pointed. "Look!" He was presenting as a prepubescent boy, thin as a blade of grass. He had cinnamon skin and black hair to his shoulders and was naked in the midsummer heat except for the red breechcloth, which Jaya had insisted he keep on.

The parade of fan masters was finally passing through the market gate. They began to form a ragged line on the city side of the Chrysanthemum Bridge. All wore the traditional heavy linen robes; each carried a sandalwood chest or lacquered box. Jaya counted thirty-four of them, not one less than sixty years old.

"Too many masters," she said. "Too many fans."

"Some of them need to go," said Baz, apprentice to a fan maker named Samira. He leaned against the trunk of a smoke tree beside Jaya, squeezing into a narrow patch of shade in the noonday sun.

"Go?" said Hool's cousin, Demaar, who was presenting as a chicken. He had just been expelled from the land of smokeless fire and, like many newly-exiled djinn, regarded the ways of mortals with confusion and dismay. "Go where?"

"Leave the city," said Baz. "Retire."

"Or die," said Hool.

"Mahir's hands shake," Jaya squirmed against the truck of the tree, rubbing an itch. "She's lucky to have a fan at all this year. Last week she ruined an ivory guard stick—three days of carving for nothing." Jaya thought of the designs she might have made on that ivory: kiwi vine and curved daggers. "They should make room for us. It's time for new masters, new ideas."

"If the court doesn't come down soon, they will go," said Hool. "It's hot as a baker's kitchen by the bridge."

Jaya thought Hool might be right. The guildsfolk seemed to shimmer under the cruel sun. "They are late," she said.

"Herself is always late for the judging," said Hool. "She doesn't care anymore."

"Not about the masters," said Baz.

"Or painted fans," said Hool. "Or anything, really, but peach wine and candied figs."

"They will care about my fans," muttered Jaya.

Baz snickered.

"They who?" said Demaar. "Hool, these people talk so fast!"

"Them. The law clowns and skywatchers and clerks of the walk." Jaya felt her cheeks burn. "Yes, even Taurean—the High Constable Herself."

Hool began to shapeshift as he crawled toward the river on all fours. The skin on his back hardened into bony plates, formed ridges. "There are eggs smarter than the High Constable Herself," he said. His legs were scaly stubs. His turtle's head pointed at the castle like a thumb. "Hardboiled eggs."

"Nobody wants more fans." Baz laughed. "Jaya's right. Too many fans already."

Demaar the chicken fluttered his useless wings. "Listen!"

Jaya heard it then: an iron groan that made her teeth ache as the castle doors swung open, then the bamboo twitter of flutes and the bronze splash of a gong.

"Too many fans, Jaya?" The turtle's hindquarters stretched and he tilted toward the river. "Too many masters in your way?" Hool slipped into the dark water.

Jaya felt a thrill of fear and thought to call him back, but was afraid to draw the attention to herself. Besides, how could she thwart the will of djinn?

As the court processed toward the castle side of the Chrysanthemum Bridge, the fan makers hunkered painfully to their knees. One by one they opened their boxes to show the utmost fans they had brought. Their positions had been determined by jury; Patri had secured second in line; Mahir was third. They had the best chance of having the High Constable Herself chose one of their fans; Taurean rarely dawdled over the judging, and on a day this hot she would want to get it over with. Samira, Baz's master, was twenty-fifth.

The musicians fell silent as Taurean mounted the bridge; her court followed. As she approached the guildsfolk, Jaya held her breath. Although Mahir's fan was unfashionable, Jaya had no doubt it was a masterpiece of the old style. The blue of the dragonfly's wings spoke to the sky and the green of the cattails was as cool as the river. The leaf was almost translucent and, when it was spread, the ivory slips that supported the silk were as fine as Jaya had ever seen. Despite herself, Jaya hoped Taurean would take Mahir's fan and not Patri's. That honor would bring merchants and bankers to the doors of their studio until there was frost on the pumpkins.

Jaya glanced away from the procession and shaded her eyes against the glitter of sunlight on water. Where was Hool?

"Taurean never chooses the first in line," Baz explained to the chicken. "It would seem too vulgar."

The High Constable Herself lingered over Patri's fan. She actually took it from its box, but then let it rest on her left cheek momentarily.

Jaya gasped. "She's not going to take it."

"How do you know?" said Demaar.

"Fan language," said Baz. "Closed fan to the left cheek means no. To the right means yes."

Jaya parted the drooping leaves of the smoke tree for a better view. "She's moving on."

"You talk with fans?" asked Demaar.

"To say all kinds of things," whispered Baz. "Kiss me, leave me, forgive me…"

Jaya could see flashes of green as the High Constable Herself spread Mahir's cattail fan and held it to the sun to shade herself.

"… I hate you, I love you."

Taurean spoke to her chief skywatcher and he nodded. Then she held the fan in her right hand in front of her face.

"She has chosen—it's over," said Baz. "The fan says follow me."

Even from this distance Jaya could see the master's smile as she closed the lid of the box that had held the prize fan. Then Mahir craned her neck at the crowd on the riverbank and Jaya realized that the master was looking for her. She shrank into the foliage, filled with foreboding. Had she made a true wish? What was it?

The High Constable marched past the line of masters, fanning herself carelessly against the midday swelter. Her retinue trooped after, snatching fans from proffered boxes in their haste to keep up and return to the cool walls of the castle. Nobody took time to admire the splendid paintings on the fans they had chosen.

"Look." Demaar turned first one chicken eye, then the other toward the castle side of the bridge. "Turtle."

Jaya blinked against the brightness of the day and saw a dark blemish on the limestone pavers. A blemish that crawled toward courtiers streaming back across the bridge. A blemish that the High Constable Herself appeared not to see. At the last minute Jaya thought to call out a warning. But to who?

The High Constable Herself slipped on the turtle and fetched up hard against a stone railing. The impact knocked the fan from her hand. With a flutter of the blue of the sky and subtlest of greens, it disappeared into the river's murk.

The air seemed to buzz as the chief skywatcher leapt to his lady's side. He tried to help her regain her balance but she pushed him away. When he stepped back and bowed low, Taurean petulantly grabbed his fan and hurled it into the river. They stared at each other for a frozen second and then the High Constable Herself laughed her braying laugh. Taking his cue, the skywatcher broke into a broad smile. Taurean gave him an imperious wave of her hand and the skywatcher turned to the chief law clown behind him, closed thumb and forefinger over the leaf of that worthy's fan, lifted it over the railing and let it go. The giggling clown turned to the next in line, who turned yet again. Within minutes the surface of the river was covered with priceless fans, bleeding red and blue and yellow into the swirling waters.

The court was helpless with laughter. The crowd roared approval. Jaya felt as if she had swallowed a stone.

"Hool!" cried Demaar. "Don't leave me with these people!"

For the next few hours, Jaya jostled through the crowds celebrating the uproarious finale of the fan judging, searching for her djinn. She checked his rooms and favorite smoke houses and dice stages and dozens of taverns—even the joy hutch where they had first met. He was gone. At dusk she let herself be carried along by the stream of revelers flowing into Shining Tree Square in the Old City.

… and eighteen fan makers fainted.

Twenty-six. I was there.

Watch yourself.

Pretty fans, yes, but who for?

Skywatchers? Witches?

Fish.

Hah! Give me a taste of that.

The cobbles of the square were sticky with spilled drink and squashed fruit. The crowd closest to the river churned to get the best view of the fireworks. Jaya pushed in the opposite direction; there was room to breathe by the ring of trees surrounding the fountain.

"Jaya!"

She started. By the dim light of the phosphorescent leaves, she picked out the master at the lip of the fountain. She was sitting on the lap of a bumpy man in homespun brown.

"Mahir?"

"Is this your grandmother, girly?" The man's voice was thick.

"I'm nobody's grandma," Mahir turned and pointed a mug at him; dark liquid slopped over the edge.

"She's a master fan maker." Jaya was outraged. "She won Herself's prize today."

"Then take her, would you?" When he shifted his legs, Mahir squawked. "She's a load."

Jaya offered the master her arm and Mahir let herself be lifted off the man.

"We should go home," Jaya said.

"Why?" Mahir gestured at the city with the mug. "What's there?"

Jaya was shocked: in the two and a half years she had known Mahir, the master had ever maintained an icy sobriety. "Your bed and a soft pillow," she said. "The studio."

"Leave it." She cackled. "Who needs it?"

"You're old, you're drunk and it's dark," said the man. "Go home."

Mahir pulled a glowing leaf off a low branch, crumpled it and threw it at him. Jaya tugged her away.

As she dragged Mahir from the light of the square into the night, guilt overwhelmed Jaya. "Master, listen. I've done something... I didn't mean... please, understand..."

"Babble, babble, silly girl."

Jaya squared her shoulders as if to steel herself against a blow. "I've been with a djinn, his name is Hool, we were by the river, at the judging and he turned into a turtle."

Mahir's grip on her arm tightened.

"He swam across the river. Taurean tripped on him."

The master staggered. "A djinn, you say?"

Jaya nodded, and then realized that Mahir couldn't see her in the dark. "Yes."

For a moment, they swayed in the middle of the street, Jaya holding the master upright. Then Mahir shook herself free. "And your wish?"

"I didn't have one. I wanted my release, but he said that wasn't enough. I don't know, I don't know. Do you have to say it to wish it?" She paused. "I'm sorry." She hadn't expected to say it, but once she had she knew it was true.

"You are." Mahir tipped the mug to her lips, then coughed as if she had tasted something evil. "Have a drink?"

"No."

Mahir shrugged. "I will tell a story, one that the masters have been chewing on. Once upon a time..." She giggled. "Once there was a high constable named Tjader. This Tjader had a hobby, she made fans. Wasn't much of a constable actually, and the fans...." The master snorted. "Tjader's great achievement was living a long time. And the festival. Her idea. Outlived her—who knows why? Maybe the gift of a djinn, eh? I need to sit down." She aimed the mug at the curb. "There."

"Master, we...."

"There, silly girl."

Mahir started toward the spot and bent but lost her balance and toppled backwards, her legs shooting out. Jaya propped her up, despairing that this awful day might never end.

"We're mortal, girl. Life seems long, but it's only a moment. A moment. What you don't realize is that everything has just a moment. The castle. The city." She tilted her head back to stare into the night sky. "Maybe even the stars. And fans, oh yes. When I was your age, I thought they were forever. But Taurean's father had no use for fans. And Herself...well. You saw. We're a joke. The moment has passed."

Jaya stood before her master, looking down in horror. "What are you saying?"

"Your wish is granted, Jaya. You have the eye of a master—and the skill." She raised a trembling hand and made knifing motions to the left and right of Jaya, as if to cut that which bound them together. "I release you. Your moment begins now, Master Jaya." She sighed. "But it's not what I would have wished for you."

For most, life in the Happy City was not much different after that famous Festival of the Fans. Few took note when the guild of master fan makers disbanded, because there was no shortage of fans. Jaya saw to that, as she became one of richest merchants in the city. Her factory still makes cheap fans of paper and bamboo by the thousands, fans that even a butcher or a clown can afford.

These the people buy to toss off the Chrysanthemum Bridge each year on the last day of the Festival of the Fans.

It is said that if you give a fan to the river on that special day, your luck will change forever.

Clockwork Companion

Elsa Colón

The gearhead god of happy endings takes a look
and tells me there's something wrong with my wiring:
The carnies in my system aren't completing their circuit,
aren't getting the grin and grimace they're going for.
No one's having any fun.

I say he should just deus ex my machina, but he won't.
He suggests I find the ghost that's interfering
and put an override in place.

Thing is, I kind of like my clockwork companion
who tocks when I tick.
The time signature tattoo on his minute hand is darling.

When no other positive reinforcements come through,
at least I have him, the perfect little metal listener,
who tells the strongman to stop his pretensions
and the bearded lady her seductions.
He keeps them all in line and away from me.

My center holds because it holds nothing
more than him and me.

Call for Submission
Libby Cudmore and Matthew Quinn Martin

Princess Pumpkinbottom's Asphalt Oreos is looking for unique works of literary and speculative fiction. PPAO only publishes one-of-a-kind pieces, such as stories written on the backs of matchbooks, or novelettes where each word is individually inscribed on a grain of rice and collected in a hand-blown glass jar.

Cape Codpiece is particularly interested in epic fantasy 600 pages or longer written from a masculine, Anglo-Saxon perspective. Although open to reading works from divergent points of view, CC prefers narratives centering on the restoration of an imperialist monarchic order, usually as the culmination of a quest. Preference will be given to submissions accompanied by a quaint, antiquated map (not to scale).

Dave Eggar's Super Awesome Sleepaway Camp Anthology is seeking only the kind of groundbreaking fiction worthy to be included in an e-publication bearing the name Dave Eggar. We are especially interested in reading pantoums, odd-numbered litanies, stories told in the fourth person or in the "royal" we, as well as racist limericks about zombies.
> (***Disclaimer:** *Dave Eggar is not associated in any way with the heirs or estate of Mr. David Eggers.*)

The La-Zee-Boy Occasional Irregularity is not accepting finished works, just ideas for stories. We are particularly interested providing a platform for immensely talented writers who are unable to finish a

The Mourning Wood Review is a quarterly publication printed on only the finest vellum. We are seeking works of lamentation, grief and loss, the types of tales that express the deep hollowness at the center of our souls. Although MWR is open to all genres (except horror, crime, romance, comedy, mystery, science fiction, and westerns) we are especially interested in stories of the mytho-poetic variety or those incorporating Judeo-Christian allegory in a vague and inoffensive fashion. Also seeking wood-block illustrations (send as .jpeg).

Crazyhomelessguy publishes fiction, poetry, CNF, and random rants regardless of quality or style. Previous contributors include DeLaVega, Neckface, and that New York Times published poet who camps out in the subway and will write you a poem for a dollar.

Glazing the New Detroit is an avant-garde publication that seeks to touch you in places you might not enjoy being touched. We are interested in giving voice to writers who are not content to merely cut to the bone, but dare to saw through it with their work.

In the Buff believes that honest writing can only come from a state of total vulnerability and as such requires that all submissions be written naked. To document this process, we ask that contributors include a notarized photo of themselves writing in the nude. Upcoming theme issues include *Pantsless Poetry, Shirtless Shorts*, and *Flash by Flashers*.

The Biannual Quarterly is no longer accepting submissions for this reading period.

Fun with Needles is seeking stories revolving around the themes of Heroin Abuse, Tattoos, and/or Knitting. New contributors should strongly consider submitting to one of our regular columns: *Pattern of the Month, Autoclave*, or *Shooting Gallery*.

Orbs

Jeff Kass

Edward McConnigle believes he's addicted to his wife's ass. He finds himself increasingly wanting to do nothing except look at it, or touch it. He can't stand when he's not near it. If Wendy's rear is not circling within fifteen feet, it becomes difficult for Edward to concentrate on the tangible world in front of him and he must flee as quickly as he can to the fantasy universe he's paid to create.

None of this is particularly harmful.

Far better to be obsessed with his wife's ass than repulsed by it.

Over the years, Edward believes, his anxiety has even led to several breakthroughs at work. Nonetheless, because he gets paid to understand the psychology of addiction, to dance on the line where obsession meets madness, today—as Wendy turns thirty—Edward worries he's lurching toward trouble.

He types, his fingers beetling hard clacks across the keyboard. In his imagination the Oak Giant Moltaw grows and extends his enormous reach, stretching toward a sky roiling with storm, toward a jagged icy mountaintop and a buried ore-mine. The creature—part tree, part human, mostly demon—tugs his heavy root-feet from the ground and rumbles across a corpse-strewn canyon. In the corner where Edward sits, the light is dim. The communal office itself is bright, loud with color, but Edward has unscrewed the florescent bulbs above his head and has no pictures, no posters or cartoons pinned to the corked walls near his desk. No windows either. He listens to no music and thinks of his wife's ass, how round it is, how firm, and a volleyball-sized globe forms in Moltaw's colossal wood hands. The giant paws it, massages it. Edward's colleagues behind him laugh at some silly joke and he ignores them. They ask him what he wants to order for lunch and he doesn't answer. The globe in Moltaw's hands is on fire, bright like a thousand boiling suns. Edward's fingers are running across the board, sprinting now, fast, fast, faster.

In the shadowy pith of the earliest parts of the morning, a time when his misgivings could keep him fidgeting and wary, the sound that soothes Edward is the tapping of Wendy's fingers against her own keyboard. He can barely hear it. Her bulky desktop sits weighty in the den down the hall from their bedroom. Still, to Edward, the faint music of her typing—the only noise audible in their rustic wood-and-glass home secluded deep amidst a grove of moist and hairy pines—is a lullaby, an aural massage shepherding him peacefully, at last, to sleep.

She wakes at three a.m. each night to write, burning a light in their dark den. Edward has no idea what she's writing and she's never told him. She could be working on promotional copy for work, or a novel. Whatever she's writing, the act is crucial in sustaining their relationship. Their routine is consistent. They eat something meatless she's cooked, read or watch TV, split a bottle of wine, hit the bedroom around ten-thirty, more often than not have a kind of sex the teenage Edward never imagined was possible, then she falls asleep and he can't.

Her breathing irritates him. It isn't snoring exactly—no honks or wheezes—but it's loud enough to crawl into his head and keep him awake staring at tree-shadows, thinking of new ways to torment his games-clients.

Games-clients: that's what the executives at Broken Window call the customers who buy the videogames Edward and his cohorts design. But Edward and the other designers, Richard and Corrina, they just refer to the game-buyers as *heads*.

When they write programs they write with a nineteen-year-old boy in mind, a kid out of high school but not in college, maybe pumping gas or slicing tomatoes at a deli. They want him staying up all night, staring at a television or computer screen, trying to figure out their inane and complicated sequences until his brain matter coagulates like bubblegum. They want him hooked. That's what Edward's orbs are about.

His game, *Wicked Wizard*, is the company's top seller. Every eighteen months when a new version debuts, people line up outside stores to buy it. The orbs are the key. Edward thinks of himself precisely as if he were a drug dealer, has even studied movies like *Scarface* and *New Jack City* so he can emulate drug-dealing tactics.

The orbs in the early levels of the game are easy to find. Their value is immense, but fleeting. Once a head finds an orb, he gains nearly limitless power. He can build or destroy. He can kill or bring back to life. In the edition with the Parental Advisory sticker on the cover—the one that outsells the cleaner version ten units to every one—he can also disrobe and fuck pretty much anyone he wants, of either sex, and the hermaphroditic multi-sexed creatures too.

The orbs last only scant minutes. Once their power wears off, heads frantically search for the next fix, for an orb that can last longer and allow the player to mate with even more bizarre creatures. The more a head wants an orb, the harder the orbs become to find. As a head progresses through the game, he'll discover many fake orbs—glowing teases that are hollow and useless. Real orbs grow nearly impossible to attain. That's what keeps Edward up at night, thinking about how he can lead heads right up to the edge of snaring the perfect all-powerful orb, then yank it away just before they clutch it. In the shadows flitting across the bedroom, he see swords and chests of ore and camels, wars, and great burning fortresses, and cavernous ravines. His mind whirls with all of it, pitching to the beat of Wendy's irritating breathing, and he's anxious and nauseous and ready to smash his head through the plate-glass window until, finally, Wendy stirs, kisses him, and clambers out of bed.

Perhaps it's because Edward types on a keyboard all day and relishes the idea of someone else doing it; or perhaps it's because he can't hear Wendy breathing from the other room; either way, within minutes of her beginning to type, he'll drift off, his own breath raspy, but rhythmic.

Edward loves Wendy, though he considers her a freak. Not so much for the nocturnal writing, but for the other stuff, the kitsch she thinks is so clever and spreads around the house like a disease. She brings home a new coffee mug or doormat, or towel, or throw pillow at least once a week. Each time, the item will boast some ostensibly clever slogan like "I'm only a bitch on days that end in A-Y" and Wendy will be giddy, like a kid presenting at show-and-tell.

"You'll love what I found," she'll say. "Isn't it hysterical?"

Yeah, he'll say, it's hysterical. But he'll think: Freak. I married a freak. He's got his own oddities too, of course, has to have them in order to concoct so many orb-gathering scenarios. Still, Wendy's schlock is bothersome. For one thing, it takes up a lot of space. The refrigerator is covered with magnets and the cupboards overflow with mugs and shot glasses. Edward can't turn around in the living room without knocking a throw pillow off a personalized director's chair. Half-a-dozen doormats line the front vestibule like a set of synthetic railroad ties.

"Don't you think you're obsessed?" he ventured once.

"Obviously, I'm obsessed," she said. "But who am I hurting? I laugh when I see this stuff. Don't you like when I'm in a good mood?"

Obviously, he likes that. And there's the question too of her ass. When Wendy isn't working, writing in the middle of the night, or buying kitsch, she's at the gym. The ass in question could be featured in art museums. It's a dream, really, a computer nerd like him sleeping with a woman as muscular as Wendy. Richard and Corrina, co-geeks who only ever sleep with each other, constantly remind him to appreciate his good fortune because it might not last.

"She just wants to know the secret of your orbs," Richard teases him.

"She's just another dopehead," Corrina says. "Once she builds up her tolerance for you, she'll move on to the next drug."

Edward agrees with Corrina. He's rich, no doubt, has been profiled twice in *The Northwest Times* because of his game's popularity. At heart, though, he's still the same dweeb the girls laughed at in high school. Still the same chunky pale kid who spent his summers playing *Dungeons & Dragons* by himself, sitting legs-crossed on the screened-in porch, inventing new ways to make the game feel more real. Wendy probably flirts with a ton of square-jaws at the gym. She also knows all the players on the SuperSonics, has their phone numbers in her personal Rolodex, yet, improbably, keeps coming home to Edward. So what if she buys a bunch of knick-knacks? He intends to hold onto her as long as he can.

That means he has to keep letting her think there's a better high to be discovered in Edward McConnigle. As long as she keeps taking hits, one day she'll reach it. This is also the dark secret of the orbs. Edward lets his game-clients believe there's an ultimate rush out there—an orb of undrainable force that will let them command and fuck their every desire. Yet no such orb exists. The quest is eternally fruitless and, therefore, never-ending. It's a bait-and-switch deal, sure, but so what? It's the journey that matters. People are never happy when they have everything they want. There has to be an unobtainable grail to keep them motivated. If there's nothing left to reach for, what's the point of living?

Edward's building an army of Seeklings.

One at a time, each creature sprouts like a thin, blue weed. Some are tall. Some are taller. Two have no knees. He duplicates them. Copy, paste, copy, paste. His fingers scamper across the keyboard like a herd of wildebeests. The Seeklings number in the thousands. They ring the shores of a lake made of liquid silver. Upon the order from High Commander Raven-Solaris, they dip their right arms into the lake and pull them out as gleaming swords. Then the general, mounted on his Ur-steed, issues another order and the Seeklings dip their left arms into the lake and pull them out as scimitars.

Edward's fingers stop.

He doesn't know what to do with the Seeklings.

They will all die, but how?

Will the lake rise up and drown them?

Will Moltaw stomp them into the earth? Will the silver encasing their arms creep across the rest of their slim elfin bodies and freeze them into inert statues? Edward feels like an inert statue himself. This plotline stinks.

He stares at the screen. Without looking he reaches for the cup of soda on his desk and gulps, spilling half of it down the front of his sweater. It's a purple V-neck Wendy bought him to try and liven up his wardrobe of drab T-shirts. His wrists ache from typing. He doesn't think, shakes them loose. Corrina notices.

"Step away from that keyboard," she says.

"It's not that," Edward says. "I'm fine, I swear. Just stuck. I don't know what to do with the Seeklings."

"I saw what I saw. You know the drill. Away from the keyboard. Now."

"I'll get the ice," Richard says. "Edward, this is serious. Don't screw around."

"Fuck the blue elves," Corrina says. "You're grounded."

Carpal tunnel. The bane of a programmer's career. Long ago, Corrina, Richard, and Edward made a pact. If any of them spots anything remotely approaching repetitive stress symptoms in any of the others, there's no argument. The designer is removed from his or her keyboard for seventy-two hours. Ice on the wrists. Fingers on forced vacation.

"You guys, I'm on deadline. The game has to be done in two weeks and I've got this stupid party tonight. Come on, let me just jam a few more hours. I'll quit before the party and take time off, promise."

"You're done, Wizard man. Pull the fucking plug."

A bag of ice smacks into the back of Edward's head and Richard hands him a paper towel. "Clean your shirt," he says. "You look pathetic. When you're finished, you know what to do with the ice. Twenty minutes on each wrist, then elevate. You've got enough damn elves. What do you have, fifty thousand by now?"

It's true. Edward's been building more Seeklings because he doesn't know what to do with the ones he already has. A whole nation of them stand around the rim of a lake like putzes, so crowded against one another they can barely move their scrawny blue elbows, and they're waiting for orders that will never come. Edward might as well admit what Corrina and Richard already know. He's reached a dead-end.

His recent game-writing has been awful: level after level of stock drooling villains and unsexy hermaphrodites. He suspects any heads who camp out overnight to buy his next edition will be furious. They'll dash his game into the gutter and crush it with steel-toed boots. With Wendy too, he feels stuck. He wants her to be excited to see him, but he's lusterless. He's losing her because he's afraid of losing her.

There's too much pressure to create a new high.

If there's any consolation to how he's feeling, it's the Sonics tickets. They're by far the best perk of Wendy's job as the team's Public Relations Director. Floor level. About halfway up. Above the tunnel where the players enter from the locker rooms.

Edward's never been much of a sports fan but Wendy's dragged him to so many games, he's grown attached. The Sonics are terrific. They play tenacious defense and are led by a pair of young and energetic stars: the perpetually trash-talking Gary

Payton, and the spectacular Shawn Kemp—the Reign Man—who specializes in thunderous dunks. Edward was so inspired by one of Kemp's throw-downs, he created Moltaw in tribute. The mammoth walking tree guards Darkland Forest the same way Kemp defends the basket. If a head's too slow to reach an orb, Moltaw will snatch it with his monstrous branch-hands and hurl it to the ground, shattering its shell into millions of shards, leaking its magic into the unforgiving night.

The rest of the Sonics aren't hapless Seeklings either. Weathered veterans like sharpshooters Ricky Pierce and Eddie Johnson score in bushels, and the remaining roster forms a quirky but winning cluster: Michael Cage with his Jheri curl, the ugliest jumper in the league, and an insatiable thirst for rebounds; the chattering mini-dynamo Dana Barros; the reliable floor-general Nate McMillan; the long-armed sleepy-eyed Derrick McKey; and, finally, Big Smooth Cool Jazz Sam Perkins.

It's hard not to love the Sonics, the way they've reached the Western Conference Finals by buckling down on D and offering a different hero each triumph. With nothing to do and his wrists growing numb from the ice, Edward gushes about their attributes.

"Think about it," he says. "We live in a city full of geeks just like us. Everybody's full of irony. Everybody wants to drink coffee all day and sneer at everything. When was the last time Seattle was this close to winning anything athletic? Kemp, Payton, Cage, Perkins, Game Seven. These guys are incredible. Wendy can get you tickets."

"Shut up," Corrina tells him. "We write games all day, you think we want to watch another one?"

"Bunch of overgrown jockstraps," Richard says. "They're the same jerks who beat us up in middle school, and now you're rooting for them? Talk about a sellout."

"You don't understand," Edward insists and something in him wants to fight for this team he's chosen to adore. He knocks the ice off his wrists and gestures with both hands. "It's the quest. Just like we talk about. These guys are always chasing one moment of pure symmetrical grace—one shot or one block, one pass that stands the universe on its head and spins it."

"Wow, when you put it like that," Corrina says, "it makes me want to sleep with them. All of them. Those perfect bodies. That would be the quest for me."

Richard laughs and Edward knows what Corrina said is only funny because Richard has no fear she'll ever undertake such a quest. She'll never sleep with anyone but him and he knows it. She won't grow tired of screwing him on the floor under the huge slab-table in the conference room because it's so convenient, and Corrina's big on convenience.

Still, the remark unsettles all three designers. Makes them aware of their own less than hospitable bodies. The three are fleshy after all, and chalky, and a bit greasy in some areas. How can they not be? They spend long hours in front of their screens, banging keys, or drinking huge Cokes and staring into space and conjuring. At some point midday, they order in heaping platters of lunch, usually Thai, but sometimes Mexican or Italian, which they proceed to spread out on the slab-table that Richard and Corrina often interface beneath before they go home. For hours after lunch, on and off, they keep eating and working until the food grows soggy and both their brains and stomachs are fried. They're a trio of doughy, pear-shaped computer nerds, two male and one female, and, physically, they know damn well they'll never be able to catch the universe's attention, let alone spin it on its head.

All that's fine for Richard and Corrina, Edward thinks, because they've got each other. They sit in thick swivel chairs and write code all day and if they make major breakthroughs, or even minor ones, they high-five and check to see if the conference room's empty so they can screw. But Edward has to compete with outsiders, with bouncers and waiters and strippers who pump up at the gym with Wendy and, surely, admire her otherworldly ass. The place is wall-to-wall mirrors. She must, at least at intermittent moments, admire her own glorious gluteus too. What does she think when she compares it to his pale, flat, flabby one?

Edward's contemplated all this before. Many times. At least he's probably richer than the waiters, bouncers, and strippers. His ass might be flat, but his wallet bulges. What he hasn't thought about so much is the NBA superstars. He knows Wendy's friends with them, sure, but they're sort of co-workers. Isn't it taboo to hook up with a co-worker?

Not that *his* two co-workers don't hook up all the time. He stumbled over them once when he skipped into the conference room with hopes of procuring a still-surviving spring roll. They weren't even embarrassed.

"That's not the last one, is it?" Corrina asked him about the spring roll as she sat up from beneath Richard, her naked breasts flopping downward like a pair of tube socks. "Because I get hungry after these interludes. I'll be starvin' like Marvin if there's none left."

That Edward (having lost his appetite) placed his spring roll back on the table hardly makes up for his otherwise disastrous physique. He's in terrible shape. Trying to convince his wife his body is more appealing than the bodies of professional basketball players is equivalent to trying to convince a nineteen-year-old stoner it's more fun to play Old Maid than *Wicked Wizard*. And the NBA guys have money. A lot more than Edward. Plus, he's stuck. He's got two weeks to send his final edits to production and now he can't work for three days and he's got fifty thousand useless Seeklings. The wage gap between him and NBA players will grow even larger if his next version doesn't sell. The only remaining question is whether Wendy's proximity to these hyper-affluent Adonises also translates to screwing them. The Sonics, after all, must have a gigantic table in their conference room, and there's little doubt they'd want to bone Wendy. Sure, they probably have loads of women to choose from, but an ass like hers, which so resembles the very object they're paid to dribble up and down the floor, they'd probably reach for it out of muscle memory.

Edward, mighty designer of hermaphroditic dwarves and tumescent warlocks, bears no illusions regarding the possible dimensions of Wendy's desire. Could she be a star-fucker? Of course she could. He met her at a charity event where Sonics players were playing *Wicked Wizard* alongside kids with cancer, and her ass was the most astounding monument to geometry he'd ever laid eyes on. He'd done the gig for free because, well, jeez, it was kids with cancer—and she'd appreciated his kindness and agreed to have coffee. Then again, maybe her attraction to him had nothing to do with kindness. Maybe the coffee and the subsequent marriage were all about how on one single day, one freaky quirk in the cosmic calendar, sick kids were more excited to see him—the guy who created *Wicked Wizard!*—than they were to hang out with professional athletes. Maybe that's why he's always felt so much pressure to entice her with new titillations. Maybe deep down he's always known her attraction to him was nothing more than an opportune moment of star-aura bullshit.

Edward pushes up from his dim corner and bites a hole in the bottom of the plastic ice-bag, crunches a half-dozen cubes in his mouth. He walks over to the other side of the office. The window he never looks out. A handful of kayakers on Lake Union. For maybe twenty minutes he watches them. One couple in an orange two-seater seems to enjoy pausing at houseboats as if inspecting them. They paddle for thirty or forty yards, stop for a minute at each residence, then start up again, each time paddling in unison, right arms raising skyward then dipping as their left arms rise. Each time the blades flip out of the water they catch a glint of sunlight so it looks like they're flashing a message in Morse code. Edward wonders if the message is for him, if the two paddlers are pursuing a dream, wanting one day to purchase a houseboat of their own. Wanting to raise a floating family.

"Elevate your wrists," he hears Richard say from somewhere behind him. "Don't forget to elevate."

Party time. Wendy's thirtieth birthday.

Entering her fourth decade, hitched to a still supposedly creative genius, Wendy Bonder-McConnigle is the head of an important department for a professional sports franchise and tonight she's swathed in a tight silver skirt that shoots skeins of light around the room like a disco ball. The result is a woman glowing, in her prime, floating on the dazzle of a life she first imagined, then successfully constructed. Her colleagues are shining too, bathing in her joy, clinking champagne flutes. Wendy seems to personify the jaunty mood felt by everyone at the party, except for Edward. With every swish-turn of her sparkled hips, another high-five clangs between friends, another arm drapes around a shoulder.

Two of the Sonics players have shown up to smile down at lesser team-employees. Eddie Johnson towers in a salmon-colored cashmere sweater—everyone calling him Eege, short for E.J., as if they've all known him since second grade—and Michael Cage is resplendent in a yellow linen suit, his Jheri curl trimmed to a neat square-shaped Afro. All Edward can think is, which one is Wendy fucking? Is she screwing them both?

He knows he's behaving like a moron, using his tender hand to sketch pictures of demented blue elves with over-large genitals on cocktail napkins and hiding them around the room. He's also drinking too much, chain-chugging rum-and-Cokes and glaring at Wendy whenever she talks to another man. He wants to be happy for his wife, but all he really feels like doing is going back to the office and generating monsters who can mutilate cartilage. He wishes, actually, he could fashion a monster version of himself. Write code that could grow him as big and strong as Moltaw so he could grab the most powerful orb he's ever created and slam-dunk it into the punch bowl, splattering acidic flames, incinerating everybody.

He downs another drink and scarfs another sandwich, a divine wedge of cream cheese and cucumber on pumpernickel. Growing up, he never tasted these kinds of mini-sandwiches, never conceived of their existence. But ever since his game began to sell, he's been invited to fancy cocktail parties. Now he's sampled them dozens of times. He doubts he'll ever grow tired of nibbling their edges, of gulping the middle in one hefty swallow. He always eats too many of them, totally disregarding whether there's enough for everybody else. More than the car with the leather interior, more than the sharp-looking house in the pines, this is the one marker of success he can never go back to living without—the cream-cheese sandwiches from God.

He thinks of his game not selling, of his fame aura disintegrating. He gobbles four more.

Edward kills two hours. He glares at Wendy; he wishes he could incinerate people; he tires of rum and Coke and guzzles champagne; he shovels mini-sandwiches into his mouth and spreads a flourish of dirty pictures around the room. Then, at last, the big moment arrives: the unveiling of the group gift. One of Wendy's friends—a second-in-command named Janet—initiates a whole showy production: music off, lights low, glasses high, everybody gathered in a circle. Edward wants to leave. Draws three more pornographic elves. Eats another sandwich.

"Everybody knows," Janet begins, "what a fabulous season the team's having, and just for the record, the basketball players aren't doing badly either."

Everybody laughs. Even Cage and Eege. Morons, Edward thinks. All of them.

"Our job is to present our players to the public, and we all know everybody likes to be liked. I have to believe some of the success on the court this year owes itself to the enthusiastic support of the community, and it's people like Wendy who bust their tails every day to create that support."

Edward cringes at the notion of Wendy busting her tail. And is he just imagining it, or is there a collective intake of breath by the rest of the males at the party too?

"The thing about Wendy is she's the kind of leader who when somebody's sick or having an off day, she's always there with a hug, a cup of tea, some calm advice. She's like the mother we always wanted, except she's too pretty and would steal all our boyfriends."

More laughs. A few people turn toward Edward to see how he's reacting to the idea of Wendy poaching men from other women. He forces a snicker. All in good fun. It's all in good fun. Idiots.

"So, raise a glass, everyone. Boss, this is just to let you know you're appreciated. Happy Thirtieth!"

With the help of a colleague, Janet spreads out a large knitted blanket, like an afghan, or a throw. Off-white with mahogany trim, it matches Edward and Wendy's bedroom decor perfectly. Edward wonders how anyone at Wendy's office knows what their bedroom looks like. Is his wife doing Janet too? Did they party in a freak-wild foursome with Cage and Eege one night while he worked late and munched spring rolls? Did they switch partners each time a new tree-shadow flickered across the wall?

Distracted, Edward fails to register the kitschy slogan, also in mahogany, stitched into the blanket's center. It's only when the crowd titters again with its moronic laughter that he focuses on the words:

P.R. People Do It
In Public
AND
Undercover

Wendy giggles with delight and skitters her feet up and down. Edward feels his stomach buckling, the sour regurgitation of champagne bubbling toward his mouth. He reaches for more wedges of cream cheese and cucumber. Wendy does it in public?

With whom? Not him. Once, on their honeymoon in the Bahamas, they made love beneath a deserted pier. They'd stayed up all night, and walked outside to bask in a sunrise that made the sky ooze violet, like a squashed grape. That was as close to public as they'd ever come, the rest of the beach empty save for a couple seagulls, and even then Edward had been nervous.

Uneasy, like he is now.

His stomach is angry. His head spins with a vision of Wendy surrounded by a half-dozen slobbering elf-creatures, all of them leering and jostling forward to mount her. He feels a jerk beneath his ribs and a sphere of congealed mini-sandwich and champagne begins to grow inside his gut, magma-hot. The whole snarling ball feels ready to erupt when Wendy, hanging onto the huge man's elbow roughly level to her ear, brings Michael Cage over to introduce him.

"You designed the Double W?" he says, his voice much higher pitched than Edward expected. He's six-foot-ten with shoulders like the deck of an aircraft carrier. "Bro, let me shake your hand. You don't know how much time we kill on the road playing that mess. Me and Kemp. Hours, bro."

Edward stretches out his hand, but the bulb inside him shudders. Fearful of splattering the man's gorgeous suit, he angles his elbow and plunges it into the rock-hard sternum of the NBA's second-leading rebounder, shoving the giant aside just as his stomach explodes in a champagne-colored stream of cream cheese, cucumber and pumpernickel. For a long moment, his vomit arcs across the room, smacking like a cluster-bomb in the middle of Wendy's new afghan, painting the words "P.R. People Do It" with a color-scheme no longer complimentary to their bedroom.

"Whoa, dude," Cage says. "Good box-out. Thanks."

"Oh, Edward," Wendy coos. "Are you okay?" And one soft hand caresses his forehead, the other reaching for a nearby napkin. In mock and giggling horror, Janet bustles over to salvage the afghan. Otherwise, the room's party-hard momentum rolls on. Glasses clink. Palms slap each other with vigor. Edward's brain continues to spin, but his wife's hand feels warm against his skin. He smiles as a cartoon elf-groin angles to swab his lips.

*

Later, after almost everyone has left and Edward has stopped eating and is mostly sober, long after Wendy has finished swabbing puke from his face and clothing, Cage comes by to talk to him again.

"We get frustrated with your game sometimes," he says, his eyebrows pinching together tightly, "like, sometimes we think you're just messing with us, that there's no such thing as a super-powerful orb. Payton says that's what it is, for sure. The Great Orb doesn't exist. But me and E.J., we see it different. We think if you look hard enough, if you keep searching, it's out there. We got faith in you. You wouldn't clown us that bad, right?"

Edward's already apologized to Wendy forty-thousand times, but on the way home from the party, in the warm cave of his car (she driving, his forehead leaned against the seat-belt strap), he tries again. "Wendy, I—"

She puts a hand up in his face. "Don't," she says.

"I know. I'm an asshole."

"Keep knowing it then. Keep knowing it for a good long while."

They sit together at Game Seven. Hanging from Wendy's shoulder is a handbag woven from hemp with an inscription dyed onto its body: *Today is the first day of the rest of the week.* Edward has to admit he likes that one. It gives him a chuckle. As the horn blows to end the first half, she looks at him. He looks at his shoes. She tells him she's going upstairs to check with her staff. Maybe grab a pretzel. What she means is she's headed to the press box to make sure everything's functioning smoothly.

The Sonics are losing.

Wendy isn't gone yet. "What I was thinking about was wanting to have kids," she says, one hand pulling lipstick from the handbag. "On the way to the party, that's what I was thinking about, maybe it was time for us to have kids."

Edwards looks up from his shoes, stares at her ass as she weaves toward the aisle.

Michael Cage has been awful all night.

Midway into the third quarter, Wendy still hasn't returned to her seat. Cage has missed eight straight shots and Barkley, who's already dropped twenty-seven points, is seriously kicking his ass.

Edward wonders if he injured the big man's ribs with his pre-puke elbow-jab, and he's overwhelmed with guilt. All these crazed and disappointed people at the game feel to him like the essence of the whole city of Seattle, its emerald soul tucked into the uppermost corner of the country. It's not just a horde of computer geeks either. Edward can see people who build airplane wings at Boeing, loggers in their checkered shirts, maybe the guy who owns the kayak rental place. The crowd is an earth-blue rollicking that shakes the arena floor with its stomp, a rounded wave yelling itself hoarse, urging Cage to do something—*just grab one damn rebound, for crissakes!*—anything to slow Barkley. Has Edward's ill-timed elbow dashed the hopes of the entire Puget Sound region just at the crucial moment when a single home-court victory would grant their long-suffering legions entry to the NBA finals?

The prospect horrifies Edward and he doesn't care what Corrina says. He's going to root his heart out, pour whatever mystical power resides within him into spurring the team to victory. Anything he can do to atone for his elbow, for his puke, he'll do it. Tonight, Edward's a jock-sniffing hometown fanatic.

Wendy's back. "It's hard up there," she says. "The whole room's depressed, even the reporters. People were so excited. I think everyone thought we had a chance."

Edwards reaches for her. Puts an arm around her shoulder. "I'm sorry," he tells her again. "We do have a chance. We still do."

The Sonics mount a comeback. Eddie Johnson leaps off the bench on fire. Every time the ball leaves his hands, it ruffles the net clean. He's carrying the team, the city. Edward can feel the energy of trees and ocean and Space Needle and lake and latté and rain and grunge and computer and airplane and bookseller and hiker and mountain, all of it, cresting. He can feel Wendy's unbounded joy as she leaps to her feet after each Sonics basket and her enthusiasm is somehow rounding and solidifying into her ass, beautifying it more. He suspects somebody in Tacoma will soon declare it a state landmark.

With twenty seconds left in the period, the Sonics tie the game and Phoenix ushers the ball up court. KJ to Barkley, inside to Chambers, back to KJ, and Edward scrunches his eyes tight, attempts to will the oak-strength of Moltaw into Cage. *Grab the ball*, he chants under his breath. *Grab the ball, own it.*

KJ to Chambers again. Chambers backs in on Kemp, then kicks the rock to Barkley. His bald head glints in the spotlight, wide open for the three. The crowd groans—a collective death of hope—but then, lunging from the tangle beneath the basket, it's Michael Cage. His long hand—which Edward realizes, he never did get to shake—morphs and expands, grows into a huge impenetrable mouth.

Barkley's shot is swallowed like a harmless mini-sandwich.

Cage spits the ball to E.J. One second left before the buzzer. One dribble and then from sixty-five feet away—three-quarters the length of the court—the shot launches. The player—for the moment without name, without space or time or memory— follows through with his shooting hand aloft like a flag.

The buzzer sounds with the ball rising.

It floats upward through the arena's scoreboard lights like a silent satellite, like Wendy's globe-ass, incandescent, dazzling.

Edward is directly behind it as it leaves E.J.'s fingers. His eyes and spirit soar in the wake of its flight and he sees kayaks. Forget the swords. Forget the scimitars. Fifty-thousand Seeklings plunge both arms back into the lake and pull them out as paddles. Pairs of them together wade into the water and their blue legs form each half of a small sleek boat. Twenty-five–thousand two- Seekling kayaks scoot in unison toward the center of the lake. Edward sees it. If a head can keep all twenty-five-thousand boats paddling in symmetry then the greatest orb in history will spout from the silver lake and levitate above the Seeklings. For a long minute it will hover and bathe them and then it will suck all of them into its core and the rest of the lake too and they will roll in a giant silver-blue mass straight over Moltaw and keep on rolling. They will crush every hissing Darkland Demon and build from their ashes an emerald heaven.

The city quiets its rumble.

Players on both teams peer upward.

Edward grabs Wendy's hand. It feels to him like he's clutching the palms of everyone in the arena, hugging the entire Pacific Northwest. It's the highest level of play. The grace Edward thought could never be attained.

Barkley knows the truth before the shot falls and shakes his bald head in disgust.

The sound the ball makes is swish.

Dragon's Chalice

A Story in Verse for Dragon-Mad Duncan
Michaela Roessner

A gilded dragon sleeps upon her massive golden hoard
    Deep within dank labyrinths of caves.
A jewel-encrusted flagon is her treasure most adored,
    Dived for, reaped from beneath the ocean's stormy foam-
    flecked waves.

Like her vast repository, Dragon glints and glimmers.
    When she slithers 'mongst her coins you can't tell her from
    her gold.
Scales lapping coils, like engraved doubloons they shimmer,
    Dragon disappears amidst the treasure she enfolds.

In a distant city, a youthful, bankrupt lord
    Boasts of labors perilous he thinks that he could brave.
Speaks of sword-skill prowess; talks of great reward,
    Silly, feckless, reckless, foolish misdirected knave.

As he keeps on gambling, as he throws the dice,
    He forestalls his loss, forestalls his debts to the other men.
For he's heard a legend of a chalice beyond price,
    Stored within a dragon's fabled hidden treasure den.

Off the princeling goes to seek the reptile
    To slaughter or perhaps just to enslave.
He'll win the cup with strength, with heart, with predatory guile,
    His land, fine name and castle he swears that he shall save.

He passes over deserts. He crosses ocean waves.
    He searches high. He searches low. He searches marsh and
    fen.
He finds a lovely island, much pock-marked with caves,
    One moonlit night he spies the pit that leads to Dragon's den.

Golden chains like gilded rain the damp cavern festoon,
    Bejeweled rings befit for kings are scattered all around.
Prince can scarcely make his way, ankle-deep in stamped doubloons,
    But for all his clinking clanking, Dragon's nowhere to be found.

So filled with glee, Lord does not see bones ground down deep among the littered gems.
    His gaze shifts upward and he spies the chalice
Set on a mound—a graceful cup, a lovely stem; a precious, jewel-encrusted treasure
    Worthy—oh so worthy!—of braving Dragon's malice.

Stay your hand! Don't pick it up! Oh, do not play the fool.
    That goblet by the serpent's most adored.
Don't doom yourself, take coins instead
    For from that very cup the Dragon's favorite drink is poured.

He falls down hard upon his knees,
    He can't resist the cup's allure—it is so fine and rare.
He risks it all. Hands grasp and seize,
    And as he rises up from theft he meets the golden Dragon's stare.

A slash of fang, a gash of claw, 'ere he can draw his sword.
    His soul leaks out. He sighs with sorrow as his life abates.
Dragon presses chalice to the oozing veins of Lord
    And with the princeling's blood, her constant thirst she sates.

So listen, lads—be brave! Be bold!
    But forswear greed. Think first and let some dangers pass.
Don't risk your life for feckless gold
    Or your blood might someday come to fill a dragon's glass.

Dinah

Matthew Quinn Martin

I met Dinah about a decade ago; crime wasn't exactly a lifestyle for us back then, more of a hobby. I had this job driving cars cross-country, and was using it to shuttle big bags of painkillers from one city to the next. If ever I got caught my excuse was going to be, "Hey, it ain't my car." Luckily I never had to use it, because it would have gotten me about as far as the county jail. I was a little north of nineteen. Romantic, horny, head full of dreams—in short, an idiot.

The plan was to sock away as much folding green as I could, then buy a motorcycle and ride to Alaska. To get as far away from Pennsylvania as possible where people still spoke English. But as they usually do, the plan changed. Changed when I met Dinah. She was hitching on a long stretch of road just outside of Holcomb, Kansas. I spotted that crazy mop of rusty curls, upright thumb, and coltish gams—gleaming naked from combat boots to cut-off jeans—and pulled up in a gray Saturn that was bound for Salt Lake City. And never made it.

She barely looked fifteen. Couple of yellowing bruises and old cigarette-end shaped scars on her arms told me all I needed to know. Damaged, didn't begin to describe her. It was like she'd been ground to sand, stuck into a blast furnace, and come out the other side as glass—only to get shattered to a million pieces and ground back down.

As she rode shotgun, the look in her constantly shifting eyes seemed to say that some menfolk had laid a pretty heavy deal on her. I never asked which ones. Uncle? Brothers? Father? Did it matter?

When she leaned forward, I spotted a gravity knife tucked into the back of her belt and made mention of it.

"Just in case some trucker decides to get frisky," she said.

I asked her why she didn't just cut her hair short like a boy, she could pass.

"It wouldn't matter to them," she said. "Any port in a storm." And she looked like she knew what she was talking about. I should have dropped her at the next rest stop, but I was nineteen—I was an idiot.

I reckon Dinah knew the ride wasn't going to be free. So she paid up front, right at 80 mph. The only rubber involved was that gripping the asphalt, but it felt safer. No way she'd try to stick me and make off with the wheels. Not if we could crash. Maybe not your typically romantic first date, but it worked for us.

Since we had a couple of days before anybody noticed the car was missing, I figured we'd hit Vegas. I knew a guy there'd be able to unload it for me. I'd be netting peanuts, but that was the drill. We stopped for gas, and as I was filling the tank, Dinah fired up a smoke. One of mine. "Isn't that a little dangerous, darlin'?" I asked.

"Nah. Know how hard it is to get gasoline to light up?" And to prove her point she dropped the half-smoked cigarette into a puddle of gasoline. The coal-red ember winked out like she'd plinked it into a mug of suds. It was right there that I knew I was in love.

So we found my guy, Richie. And like I'd predicted he gave me the high hard one for the car. Three G's for a spankin' new station wagon. After a little haggling, I got him to toss in a shitbox import pickup to tool around in. Then I got us set up with a crappy motel just off the strip. The pool'd been condemned by the board of health, and in the morning we were woken up by strips of sunlight streaming through the six bullets holes perforating the back door. Home sweet home.

I knew the money wasn't going to last, so I talked to Richie and he said he could set me up with a new short con he'd be running. He needed fresh faces; all his usual guys had either been burned or were cooling their heels in the pokey. He'd be working it too, behind the curtain, but up front it had to be a team. I reckon he meant the girl. Dinah was still working off her share of the rent the way she'd been for the past week, but I could tell she was itching to get in on the game for real. I figured what the heck. I was sick of being a solo act.

Richie had gotten hold of an empty shop, and used his connections to stock it with some hot electronics. I worked the counter; Dinah went to hustle up customers. Turns out she had a gift for finding marks. None of the out-of-town hayseeds could resist that trusting look in her big hazel eyes. She'd separate the rubes from the rest of the herd, and send them right down the kill chute.

Man their greedy, beady little eyes would bulge when they saw the prices, all just a little too low not to at least try to limbo. They'd hand over the plastic and I'd swipe it. When it wouldn't clear, I'd scratch my head and tell 'em, "You know … it's not going through. You got another card?" And when that one failed, I'd give 'em that *aww shucks* smile. "Not gonna' go. Tell ya' what … pay cash and I'll knock off ten percent.

"There's an ATM over there," I'd say pointing to one across the street. One with a pinhole video camera pointed at the keypad. Of course the credit card machine wasn't broken. It was just sending the information to the back of the shop where Richie sat with an encoder and a stack of blank cards.

Left like that it was a pretty good con. What made it perfect was that as Dinah was boxing things up, I'd ask the mark if they lived in Vegas. Of course they didn't. If they lived in Vegas they wouldn't have fallen for this scam like dominos.

Then I'd tell them that if they were from out of state they could mail the goods to themselves and skip the tax. "You can drop it in the mail box," I'd say. "It's right across the street, next to the ATM." Then Dinah'd hand them a nicely packaged brick. They bit. Never underestimate a man's greed or desire to get laid.

We ran that one for about four days. When the heat hit simmer, Dinah and I headed back to the motel with the cash and waited for Richie to show with the cards. From there the plan was to split up and hit the area ATMs, the ones in quickie marts that connected to the grid through dial-up and usually didn't have cameras. We'd do it shotgun style, random.

Six hours went by.

Then ten.

Then a day.

I checked the store. Emptied out as planned, but still no word from Richie. So we waited. We got some cheap bubbly and played checkers and fucked. Then we got a phone call two days later, collect from Tijuana. It seems Richie had woken up covered in blood. Just not sure whose and bolted across the border till things cooled. The cards were gone. We never saw him again.

We still had most of the cash: 25K—again, peanuts compared to what those cards would have gotten us. But it was something. I stuffed it into my duffle, and shoved it under the bed. I told Dinah about Richie and then hit the shower, letting the hot water wash some of the loser-stink from my body, as I figured out what to do next; 25K would last a lot longer if there was just one of us.

When I got back out, dripping—cheap motel towel barely covering my jewels—I felt a dry desert breeze hit my wet skin. Dinah stood there, her silhouette framed by the open doorway. She had the duffle full of money in one small fist, and her open knife in the other. The truck keys dangled from her pinky.

"I left you some," she said, nodding toward the nightstand. There next to the ashtray sat a stack of bills. Two large maybe.

"Generous," I said. "More than I'd have left you."

"You'd have left me dead."

I shook my head a touch. What was I going to say? Anything would've sounded like a lie. Maybe someone from her way back had left her for dead. Left her in a ravine—bruised, scraped, choked, raped. Who knew what was in that big old closet of hers. So she was going to take some green from me that wasn't even mine to begin with—big deal. What was I going to do? Kill her for it? A lot of folks would look at a girl like Dinah and say I'd be doing the world a favor by taking her out.

Well, I've never been into doing the world favors. And it's been reciprocal. "Take it easy then," I told her as I dropped the towel and reached for my pants, still crumpled next to the bed.

"Ain't you mad at me?" she asked.

"A touch. But it's just money. I'll get more. It's you I'm gonna miss." Like I said, I was nineteen—an idiot.

Dinah huffed, probably thinking I was stalling, looking for some way to get her. When I leaned back and clicked on the tube, she turned, taking a half-step through the door, lingering.

"It'll run out, you know," I said. "Money. Luck. Time. Gonna have to trust somebody sometime."

She dropped the duffel. "How do I know I can trust you?"

"You don't," I said. "That's why they call it trust."

They say most couples split up over money. So maybe that's the reason Dinah stuck around all these years. We got married that night by a guy in an Elvis suit, wrecked to the gills on rotgut tequila. I can't say it's always been smooth sailing, but here we are, back in Vegas for our tenth anniversary. Only in America.

I heard Richie's in town too. I'm not sure if he'd even remember us. Which is going to make this a lot easier. This weekend, Dinah and I are getting ours from Richie—one way or another.

Maybe I'm still an idiot, but I'm not nineteen any more.

She Looks in a Mirror
Julia Gay

The Final Girl is boyish, in a word. Just as the killer is not fully
masculine, she is not fully feminine—not, in any case, feminine in
the ways of her friends.
—*Men, Women and Chainsaws: Gender in the Modern Horror Film*

Oh to be—
Clarissa. Cordelia. Crooning wailing howling Cassandra Cassie
Cass. Or
Yvonne. Yvette. Eva. Eve. Evy. Big breasted campy chic Elvira.
Gabriella. Ghita. Anita, mi hijita grass smeared soccer shorts
glistening sweat brow tight ponytail swinging muscled arms
elbowing rivals hugging mama pounding beers running races in
heels.
Sandra. No, Sondra.
Michelle. Mikayla. Millicent. Millie. Leigh. Lia. Layla...
You got me on my knees, Layla.
Kayla. Carly sunbleached blonde bronzed freckled jean short tank
top tan line cowboy boots honky tonk woman smelling like sweet
peach wine coolers and menthols fast pink tongue.
Jill? Not Jill. Jioni. Jin. Janelle. Joelle. Ella with brown chestnut
hazelnut brazil nut walnut shimmering hair past my shoulders
willow arms piano fingers perfect pitch and perfect tits.
Lana. Lena. Lenore. Nora. Nori.
Rina with my hair eternal tumbling night. Rena with French
braids and books pressed to chest and swishing pleated skirt.
Raina ah ha hush that fuss effortless pout lipped Afro fantastic
flowy floral tops flip flops always answering why not debate
about these things these truths that are not always self evident.

But really—
Allissa. Alisha. Alima. Alina to lean on arm punch one of the guys
tabletop flat-chested loner. Alondra. Alile. Alejandra. Aliana.

Alberta named after some great great great uncle cousin grandfather guy but can throw a punch a ball take a digger a joke even when they're not funny never funny but don't be a bitch be a man. Alma. Alva. Aliya. Aliza. Allison all I wanted was a son.

All. Is. One.

All. Is. On.

Alli. Ali.

Al.

Call me Al.

Child of the '80s

Julie L. Martin

Pat Benatar … I just don't get it.

I was your child of the '80s. You said we would do it—that love was a battlefield, to hit me with your best shot, that sex is the best weapon.

I teased my hair, I rubbed on bodies with my black spandex while dancing to those Madonna classics, I wore the black eyeliner that made my eyes water and the boys notice twice. I was fifteen once too. And I learned fast. I learned that boys that are older have fast hands as well as cars, and that daddy's little girl isn't always in bed at two in the morning. She's out the window, not restricted, waiting for that car to pull up outside.

Don't ask where I've been. I can't tell you all that, because I only have a short time to tell this story. But I will tell you that it didn't turn out the way you said it would—even though those days of Aqua Net, of stealing booze from the bar, of hopping trains on the Metro—are now a faded memory clad with black asphalt and city dust. It's just that.

I was stupid to say the least. I didn't know what I was doing. I thought you knew for me. I wanted so badly to scream out to the world, to be free—to be known and be feared. I wanted those people who had tormented me my entire life to HEAR me—and they did. They heard me well. Five hours on the band floor screaming Gypsy Road with the guys and slamming back Bud Light—making sure one of them didn't get any ideas about it. I was there. I lived it—the dream. Little paradise.

Daddy didn't yell too much when I'd turn down my stereo. Papa's Roses. I'd turn you up in my mind and turn on the thoughts—lay back on my bed and picture a life beyond that dark, dreary city. I wanted so badly to find that part of me that was missing, that part of me that didn't belong there. Hell was for children. Here was my heart. I wanted out.

And I got out.

But I don't have much time to tell this story—so I'll give it to you straight.

I ran with the big dogs ... the shadows of the night. Fire and ice—I'll do it. I was somebody's baby and a prisoner of everything.

I looked for a stranger. Prisoner of love, precious time. He was a mysterious man—and he said he would take me away from this place. Promises in the dark.

I don't get it, Pat. I was wide awake in dreamland and didn't have a clue. I was there, here, and now I'm no more. It's a tuff life. So long. So sincere. So real.

Listen
Elsa Colón

There is something in the tense
and warily expectant silence
just after the rustling of a falling fruit
that suggests a suddenly halted scuffle
between two dryads.

Siren

J.M. McDermott

Odysseus was my first. Don't let my manager suggest it was him. My Odysseus walked up the beach with his friends, and a surfboard under his arm. An olive-skinned man with hair curled and dark. Muscular, and famous, I knew him on sight. I was posing with a book I wasn't reading for the cameramen along the edge of the sand. I was alone, against the rules my parents had set for me. There I was. I believed I could sing, but it was a voice that came from deep inside of me, passed through microphones and soundboards and sound men. I never heard my voice alone in an empty room. I never sang unless I had to, for joy. It was my job, and I was told to rest my voice outside the studio.

A singer who never sings, that's me. Odysseus, the King of Thrace, a royal prince among the celluloid queens, lounging among us like a lotus eater, smiled upon all debutantes. Was he married? Was he still married? I don't know. He loved to surf. I was at the ocean, and I saw him surfing and smiled to myself. I fashioned myself a future queen. Everything else was mine. I had portrayed princesses before.

I was born beneath the lights. My mother held me up to them so often that I knew nothing else. After school I ate cereal and smiled, take after take, or posed with school clothes for catalogs and magazines. I met directors, memorized meaningful family interactions, and went home after dark to sleep in a house three times as large as the set, waiting for my mother and father to stop shouting, throwing parties, or watching grown-up things that I could not, for work. Naturally, I was convinced I could sing and sing, by a friend of my father.

I opened my mouth, and sound came out into a microphone and through it. From the speakers, they spun the hay into gold. Platinum records of music written by men with daughters my age, and my face on the cover like everything beautiful in the world. The men came to my door with signs and rummaged through the trash. I flushed everything I could. We mulched and composted. God forbid a hair—or worse: a maxi pad. They'd take anything. The more blood and sweat the better. Not snot, oddly enough.

Baby, I'm a star.

Until Odysseus asked me to sing.

Odysseus saw me because the cameras were not solely his. He walked to me upon the sand. We had never stood in each other's personal space before. He nodded. "Beautiful day," he said.

It was beautiful. The sun was halfway through the sky. The cresting waves drowned the road sounds. The perfect horizon was dotted with sailboats, surfers' laughter, and the timeless haze of summer.

I nodded.

"I saw you at the Grammies," he said.

"I didn't win," I said. It was the first thing I ever said to him.

"You should have," he said. He waved and walked away. "Your voice is too perfect to be real, as if the sea itself pours from your tongue. I had to stuff my ears to survive, you know, all that noise. Whenever I'm at concerts I wear earplugs. I didn't rush the stage like the others. I wanted to."

"Flattery," I said. I had heard so much flattery.

"Yes, but still, you didn't win. I'm sorry, I speak badly."

"No. You're fine."

"Forgive me," he said. He bowed as if to royalty and walked away from me, up the dunes to the café at the edge of the street.

I didn't turn to watch.

The shadows turned like sundials. Thirsty, I walked to the boardwalk, ignoring shutterbugs, surprised that I saw him drinking alone. My father's lawyer would kill me for this. But I thought I shouldn't be out alone, anyway, and I wasn't alone if I could sit with him a while, and speak to him. (Of course, I was never alone with all the cameras. Gangly men with their cyclopean eyes were always watching over me.)

"May I?" I said to the king.

"My pleasure," he said.

I carried two sodas. I placed one beside his beer.

"Do you always go out alone?" I asked.

"I left the crew at the hotel. I have a house here. I don't need a handler."

"I do. I'm underage, you know. I snuck out alone."

"We are never alone when we are on display. I love your voice. I heard you for the first time on a radio in Rome. I had to pull over to hear it, to stop the engine of the car and listen. You really shouldn't be out alone. There are crazy ones—the collectors of things…"

"Then take me home."

"Yours or mine?"

On-screen, I never went to his. I was a chaste girl, with kisses on the cheek and hugs at proms. I sang of love that never passed second base.

He smiled. "Which would you like better?"

I looked up to his sunscreen-stained face, his naked eyes white where the sunglasses protected him. "I don't know," I said.

We held still like that until the cars moved, and the cameramen shouted encouragement. I stood too long. It was awkward to stand here like this. I was only a child. I didn't know what I was doing. He did.

"I want to see where you live," I said. "Where do kings live?"

"Castles in the sand," he said. "We can walk there, if you like. It's not a mile away up the beach. The surf carried me here, with my board."

He lived on the water, in a condo on stilts at the beach. Inside he had surfboards, open windows and hardwood floors. I had to leave my shoes in his foyer, and walked barefoot on my toes on that hardwood.

"Sing for me," he said. He had a piano, ivory white, a baby grand shorter than the surfboards along the walls.

He played a diminished chord, a major seventh, and resolved. I knew the song. My first hit. I laughed. I opened my mouth to sing.

Nothing came out.

He closed his eyes, playing the chords. I took a breath and tried to sing. Something came out, like the sound of a conch shell against the ear, as if my chest was a conch shell, and all the water sounds poured out from me. I was the sea. I had the song of the sea.

"What is the sound of joy? Is it truly this?" he said. He closed the keys of the piano. "You were too young to know the songs of the world. Too old to continue living so beguiled."

I doubled over. I coughed to make the noise of it. It sounded like choking. Is this my voice when I project? How many machines stood between my rusty textures and the tone of the layered strings and drums?

A life lived in the lights and the cameras, what did I know of song? I lived more in empty rooms and homes carved up into camera tracks and seats on the set, sound studios where I stood alone while my father watched and spoke, a disembodied voice, from the other side of the glass.

My song is of the sea, and only of the sea. A wind like whispered waves from my lips, poured into a piano. This texture hurts my lungs, spills over me with gravel. Sand spilled from my guts. Rocks and stones and driftwood, turtle shells and desiccated seaweed.

Afraid I ran upstairs, trying to sing the songs I knew by heart, trailing beachheads.

"No song," said Odysseus, climbing after me. "None." Why did he do it to me? What had I done to him?

Into the bed, and dead sand dollars, now, like frozen coins, tumbling onto pillows.

My father and his friends had led me by the hand from stage to stage. So sure of myself, I danced upon the stage with such applause, all lie and the machinery that contained the sound they threw upon the screaming fans who rushed the boards, trampling each other for a touch of my skin. All sand. All salty sea sand. I could not sing to stop the men from following me.

Odysseus climbed the stairs, the King of Thrace that threw me against the rocks I choked upon. My voice—my horrible voice—scattered onto silken waves.

My tears, my bleeding on the rocks.

Curse Odysseus, and all the men who would drown in my arms.

Hauling Them Home
Watching the black taxis load in Soweto
Patricia Smith

The seats groan with the weight
of the day spanned across
their backs, the repeated rhythm
of labor pounding in their hands.

Of the day, spanned across
the numbing landscape of a life,
of labor pounding in their hands,
they think nothing. Is the world,

the numbing landscape of life,
enough to guide them home
as vendors pile their dying fruit
higher and higher?

Enough to guide them home,
taxis bite into hillsides,
higher and higher,
vanishing the slumped shoulders.

Taxis bite into hillsides
hauling the men we ache for,
vanishing the slumped shoulders.
The seats groan with their weight.

Jockamo
Scott Wolven

After prison, it was hard to get a job. Most work faded if they found out I'd been incarcerated. I left Maine and went down South to look for a construction job. After the hurricanes hit, I found some work in New Orleans. Running heavy equipment and driving truck. Hauling tons of ruined houses to the dump-sites. The worst was the kids' toys and the pictures. Moldy, soaked stuffed animals. That really got to me. Pictures so wet you could wring them out. There was other stuff there—dead, bloated pets, and in one house, a dead body. The kitchens were always awful. People don't realize it, the simple danger of what was in some of those refrigerators. The food had sat unprotected for months. The smell of it could kill you. Lethal air-borne bacteria. We taped the fridges shut before handling them. We wore masks and breathing tanks. Special hazard suits. We looked like we were still underwater, even though the water had receded. That work ended too. On a Friday, we got back to the big garage where we kept all the equipment and they were handing out the last paychecks. Said the disaster money had run out and good luck to us in finding new work.

I got hold of a buddy of mine, back in Maine. He was part owner of a logging operation. He sent me plane tickets. I'd fly to Cleveland, then to Burlington, Vermont. He'd been awarded a contract to supply a wood-fired power plant. I could run one of his crews, cutting delivered logs from the yard into a usable size for feed-stock, and help with that side of the operation.

I was at the New Orleans airport, at the last gate in the terminal. Two hours early for my plane. I sat in the seat closest to the flight attendant's station.

An older man walked by with a small, younger woman. They looked out the floor-to-ceiling windows at the planes. He was old from work, you could tell that about him. A short man, black and gray short hair cut at home and thick black glasses. Big hands and forearms. He moved stiffly.

The woman was handicapped and retarded, from the way she walked and held herself. Her hair was short and uneven. Almost torn, not really cut. She wore denim coverall shorts, a jumper, over a pink short-sleeved shirt. Brown corrective shoes. She balled her right hand into a fist and punched her own right thigh. Slowly, she did it again. The bruise on her thigh showed purple and blue from under her shorts and slowly, she punched herself again. She and the man stood there. They looked out the window together.

"There's the plane," the man said. He had a little bit of the bayou in his voice. He looked around and nodded at me. I nodded back. The woman punched herself in the thigh. She said something, but I couldn't hear it.

"They'll take good care of you," he said. "You're going to go on that plane right there." He pointed out the steel and glass window at the runway and the plane closest to the window.

"I can't," she said. She punched her thigh.

The man put his hand on her back. She rested her head on his shoulder and she shook as she cried. His sleeve was wet with her tears when she stood straight.

"We can't drive, honey," he said. "You think about it." He stepped away from the window and walked over and sat one seat away from me. He turned to me, as if we knew each other. "Doctors say she'll kill herself with this," he said and pretended to punch his own thigh. "Give herself a clot and break it loose and float to her heart. Then it's over." He stopped. "She used to do it once in a while, but the hurricanes were too much for her."

The woman spoke. "Since I was eight," she said. "I did this."

He bent forward and looked at the carpet. He lifted his head and we both watched the woman. She was punching herself and softly crying as she looked at the plane. The voice over the loudspeaker system announced flights boarding.

The man got up and guided the woman over to the seat next to me.

"Pardon us," he said.

"No problem," I said.

The woman looked at me and smiled as she cried. Her face was red and streaked.

"I can't," she said to me.

I nodded. "It's fine," I said.

She managed to punch herself even sitting down.

"Just watch her, okay?" the man said. He held out a dollar bill, lengthwise and creased along the center, so it was stiff.

"That's not necessary," I said.

He tucked the single into my front shirt pocket. "Buy yourself a cold beer when you get the chance. You can still get cheap beer in the Quarter, if you look around for it."

"Thanks," I said.

"Do you like the beer down here?" he said. "They used to brew Dixie beer right in the city. It was always pretty good."

"If I'm thirsty, anything cold is good for me."

"I like that beer they got from Abita," he said. "I like Andygator best, and the Jockamo, with the Indian on the bottle." He paused. "I got a cooler with a couple beers in it out in the back of the truck right now. I think I got a bottle of Jockamo in there."

"I like the Andygator," I said. "I've had that."

"Used to drink a lot of Pabst Blue Ribbon," he said. "PBRs, we used to call 'em."

"I like the can," I said. "They're good if they're cold."

"My one cousin—Steve—he got up to Michigan, chasing a woman, a while back. So I'm sittin' down here, sweatin' my potatoes off, and the phone rings. I pick it up—Hello? And the voice says Hey Cousin, it's Steve! And I said Well all right Steve, how's Michigan? And he says I had to call and tell you that the place we're eating at has a drink on the menu called the Johnny Cash and I'm having one, what do you think it is? I said Steve, I have no idea and he said It's an ice-cold PBR and I thought of you right away. I got a real laugh out of that, both because of the PBR and because I used to be such a big fan of Johnny Cash," he finished. "I was so glad he called me to tell me that."

"That's something," I said.

"It's funny," he said. "You never know when people are thinking of you."

"No," I agreed. "You never do."

"I used to drink a lot of hard liquor," he said. "Now I mostly drink beer, to keep cool."

"I try not to drink when I'm working," I said. "But afterwards I'll have a few."

He nodded. "That's the way to do it," he said. He motioned at the woman. "Sit tight with her for me."

"Okay," I said.

He stood and walked over to the counter and I heard him talking to the woman about his tickets. They wouldn't give him his money back on them.

The punching woman turned and looked at me.

"Were you here for the hurricanes?" she said.

"No," I said. "Right after."

"It scared me," she said.

"I bet," I said.

"We're doing the best we can," she said.

"Sure," I said. "It'll be okay."

He came back over from the ticket counter.

"Nothing doing," he said. He pointed at the punching woman. "She can't fly."

"I can't fly," she repeated.

"What are you going to do?" I said.

"I don't know," he said. His eyes filled up. "This is a hell of a mess." He sat down on the other side of her. The punching woman stared straight ahead.

He kept talking. "Some of the family prays for her, but I don't. Not anymore." He turned to me. "Do you know what God is?" he said.

"No," I said. "I don't."

"God is fear," he said. "Fear that something bad will happen to you, if you don't stay in good with Him." He pointed around, at the whole terminal and the rest of the world beyond. "When you've seen all this," he said, "what is there to be afraid of? There's nothing left to be scared of. When you run out of fear, you stop believing in God."

"These are hard times," I said.

He patted the punching woman on the head. "She's punched herself since she was eight years old. I can't even imagine it anymore." He raised his voice and then lowered it. "God better be afraid of me, that's all I'll say." He looked over his shoulder at a man and woman leaving the terminal. His eyes glistened with water.

"I don't know what to tell you," I said.

He shook his head. "I don't know what to tell myself either."

The punching woman was still staring at the planes. "I can't fly," she said.

"We'll drive," he said. "Tonight we'll drive to Baton Rouge and stay with Aunt Jean." He stopped. "I'll borrow some money from her and see if we can take their truck to Cleveland to drop you off."

The woman shook her head yes.

"Maybe we'll stop to see your cousins in Toledo and get some money there too."

"Yes," she said.

"And then I'll have to leave you," he said.

"No," she said. She put her arms around his neck and even as she did it, she pulled her arm off to punch herself. They sat there crying and I stood up, as if my plane was boarding.

The man wiped his snot with a stained handkerchief. "Sorry about all this," he said. "We're having a tough day."

"No worries," I said. "I've had my share of those." I nodded. "Good luck to you."

The woman looked up at me. They both stood.

"Luck forgot about us," the man said. He walked a couple steps and turned around. "Can you give us a hand getting out to the parking lot? Have you got time?"

"I've got time," I said. I had already sent my bag through and I hadn't seen any line when I'd come through security. I'd leave myself time and go back through. I took the suitcase out of the punching woman's hand and walked slowly with them, back up the linoleum grade, into the main terminal.

"I'm just right out here in the parking garage," he said as we walked across in front of the ticket counters. We went through the doors and stepped outside.

The three of us walked past the concrete pillars and crossed the street into the first floor of the parking deck. We took an elevator to the second level and got out. There was a concrete deck floor overhead, but it was open-air on the sides of the deck, with some sun coming in. He was walking toward an old pickup truck with Louisiana plates, among the rows of cars and trucks. Sportsman's Paradise it read at the bottom of the plate. The man took a key from his pocket and opened the passenger side first. The punching woman got in. He closed the door behind her. He reached into the bed of the pickup.

"Have a beer," he said. He took the white lid off a cooler, pulled out a brown beer bottle, and popped the top with an opener on his key ring. He handed it to me and popped one for himself.

He raised his bottle and clinked it against mine. "Here's to you," he said. There was an Indian on the side of the bottle. "I love those Mardi Gras Indians," he said. "With the costumes and big feathers."

I raised my beer bottle. "Better times," I said.

"Here," he said to me. "Take a look over here." He opened a tackle box behind the driver's seat. He lifted out the removable middle and underneath were two flat automatic pistols.

"That small one is a Beretta," he said. "Pain in the ass to load, but it does the job up close. The other one's a Wilson concealed carry .45. That's a man-stopper."

"Nice," I said.

"The Beretta is my daddy's pistol," he said. "Kept it in his front pocket, even in church."

"Really?" I said.

"That pistol knows how to do its job," he said. "Let's leave it at that." He sipped his beer. "My daddy had a reputation around here and people thought twice before crossing him." He picked up the black Beretta and handed it to me. The metal was cold. It was hard to imagine something so lightweight ever spitting sudden, violent death.

"That's a special heirloom," I said, handing it back to him.

"We could do a private sale right here for say, about four hundred dollars and that would give me gas money to get her out of harm's way," he said. The punching woman sat in the passenger's seat, with her seatbelt on. He talked as if she wasn't there or couldn't hear him. He talked as if I might need to carry a gun. As if he knew who I'd been, years ago.

"I'm flying out in an hour," I said. "I have no way of transporting them."

"You don't have to carry them," he said. "I'll drive with 'em and once you get settled up North, I'll drive 'em right up to you. Keep right on going after I'm done dropping her off." He paused. "Just that I need that gas money to get me on the road today."

"Right," I said.

"You might need a pistol up North," he said. "Never know what might happen up there."

"I thought your truck wouldn't make it up North?" I said.

"That's if I got her," he said, looking at the punching woman. "If it's just me, I can get out and change a tire on the highway, or do whatever's necessary."

I sipped my beer. "No need for that," I said. The planes were loud coming and going and I could see the black tarmac and the sunburned green grass.

"Suit yourself," he said. He had his beer in his hand.

"I can give you about two hundred fifty dollars," I said. "Will that help?"

"Two hundred fifty?" he said. "That's fine. That'll get me started. You can pay me the rest when you see me again." He wrote his number on a piece of paper and handed it to me. "That's my number, for when you come back down."

"That's fair," I said. "I'll probably be back in a month or two. As soon as the snow starts to fly up north." I nodded. I pulled some damp twenties out of my pocket, counted them, and handed him two hundred fifty dollars. I tore the scrap of paper he'd given to me in half and wrote the number of the office number of the wood-burning plant on it. I handed it to him. He handed it back to me.

"Put your name on the back of that," he said. "I'll forget." I did. He shook hands with me. "Good to know you," he said. "I'm Eddie Ourso." He motioned at the punching woman. "This is Lenore."

The phone rang late in the day at the yard and somebody motioned to me. I shut the saw down and took my helmet off. I walked into the office and put the phone to my ear. Snow was starting to come down.

"Yes," I said.

"Hey bud, it's Eddie from New Orleans, how you doin'?"

"Good Eddie, how 'bout yourself?"

"Hell never stops, you know, just keeps on going. Look, I got a question for you," he said.

"Go ahead," I told him.

"I got to pawn those guns, I need that money," he said. "She's back with me and I got no money for groceries." I could hear the hurt in his voice.

"Pawn 'em, Eddie," I said. "Get whatever you can for 'em."

"You sure?" he said. "I feel bad about doing it, but you understand, I'm in a tight spot here."

"No problem," I said.

"And I can't pay you back that money you gave me for 'em," he said.

"I understand," I said. "Do what you have to do. Buy me a beer when you see me."

"I will do that," he said. "Get some time off and come down and we'll go fishing and drink beer. On me." He paused. "I hate to pawn my father's gun," he said. "Selling it was one thing, but pawning it," he paused, "pawning is bad times."

"He'd understand," I said.

"No," Eddie said. "No, he wouldn't, but it's nice of you to say that. He'd have beaten me to within an inch of my life if he knew about this." He was crying now.

"Take it easy, buddy," I said.

His voice was choked off. "His grave," he said. "His grave was covered by thirty feet of water."

I could hear him crying. "Hang in there," I said.

"I will," he sobbed. "I will."

The cold and snow was everyday in Burlington. Late in the afternoon, on a Friday, I was standing in the loading yard talking to Steve, one of the yard foremen, when a Vermont State Police cruiser eased its way down the sloping entrance ramp and parked in front of the equipment shed. A plain blue cop-sedan followed right behind. A uniformed State Trooper got out of the cruiser. Another State Trooper got out of the passenger's side. He had unclipped the shotgun from inside his car and stood there, watching me and Steve, holding the shotgun. We stopped talking. A cop in street clothes and a heavy jacket got out of the plain sedan. He had pushed his coat back, as if he might need to get at his revolver. Both cars had their engines running.

"Are you armed?" the street clothes cop said to me.

"No," I said.

"Come over here," he said. "Put your hands on my car and spread your legs."

The one uniformed cop spoke to Steve. "Go on about your business," he said.

"What the hell's going on?" Steve said.

"Get out of here or I'll thrown you right in the back in cuffs," the other trooper said. Both troopers were older. Steve walked into the shed, headed back to the fuel and feed-stock unit.

The troopers frisked me, took my pocketknife and put cuffs on me. They loaded me in the back of the plain cruiser. The street clothes cop got in and we pulled out of the yard, onto the highway. Headed south as the sun was going down under the snow clouds. He looked in the rearview mirror as he talked to me.

"Do you want to talk?" he said.

"I have no idea why I'm here," I said.

He held a photograph against the dividing grate. It was a still photo from a surveillance camera. It showed me and Eddie Ourso, standing, leaning on his pickup truck. I was handing him the black Beretta.

"What did he do?" I said.

"I'd rather not say," the cop said. "Right now, we're interested in what you did."

"I didn't do anything," I said.

"Sure," the cop said. "You think about it. Maybe you'll feel like talking at the station." He sipped from a coffee cup. "From the looks of your record, I'd think about talking."

The cuffs were tight on my wrists and every bump hurt, as I rode with my arms behind me. A car went past going north, tires crunching the snow. The uniformed troopers were behind us in their cruiser.

"He's singing his head off down in Louisiana," the cop said.

Lake Champlain was on our right as we drove and the sun shone faintly pink and purple, almost blue onto space between the scattered snow clouds. The colors reminded me of her. I thought of everything all at once—Eddie and Lenore and that we all bruise ourselves constantly and that the time in front of me was just a series of bad things that hadn't happened yet. That my bruise from years ago had broken loose and was floating through me, looking to clog the veins and arteries of my life.

"We know your record," the cop said. "You just found a loophole and got out. Shitty prosecution." He sipped his coffee as he drove. "We'll get you for the full-maximum on this one."

" I didn't do anything," I said.

"I doubt that," he said. "Maybe you'll talk at the station. Maybe the smell of that room will remind you of inside."

"I remember what it was like inside," I said.

The cop kept talking, like all cops do. I stopped listening. I wondered what Eddie had done, to get himself into such a jam. I sat cuffed in the back, calm. Waiting for the station and the room and their lies and pressure. And release.

Reruns

Jessica de Koninck

Right in the living room
Jack Ruby whips out a pistol
and shoots Lee Harvey Oswald

who doubles over, falls to the floor.
Again and again the scene repeats
in black and white. Anchormen in light

shirts and dark ties pontificate
while sweating televangelists predict
damnation. James Cagney takes

a bullet too only he keeps talking.
On a different channel he sings. He dances.
Ruby stretches. Oswald collapses.

Life might be safer out in space if only
the shuttle would not explode
during breakfast, and again

after dinner and then before bed.
School Teacher, Astronaut, Indian Chief.
Starship Enterprise never blows up,

even at warp speed. Spock can
sort things out. Vulcans are part
prophet, part angel. They rely on intellect,

not feelings, and most of the time
sex is no problem. Except that
one episode with the parallel universe,

the good Spock and the bad Spock.
Hard to tell one from the other,
but God must like Spock.

Though I don't believe God
watches that much TV. Maybe
the *Twilight Zone* or the *Soprano*s.

I could avoid hitting
the remote and seeing those same
sorry reruns, no reality shows,

no MASH medevac helicopters
transport wounded GIs
across Korea. No smoke,

no screams. No towers
crumble as if in slow motion:
first one, moments later, the other.

Family Secrets
Linda K. Sienkiewicz

I'm frozen, unable to utter a note, my fingers wrapped tighter around the cordless mic than if it were Jim Morrison's dick. Razor yanks the cord on his bass from the amp while shaking his head, but Dougie keeps banging away on his guitar, oblivious to the bad vibes, his head down, long black hair tangling in the strings. It isn't that I forgot the words to our new song, "Use Once and Destroy"; it's the image that materializes in front of me, as if conjured by the hand-waving audience, of Mother climbing into the back of a Mercedes with tinted windows with that idiot gigolo, Sylvester.

When I had delivered the cake for the retirement party Mother was catering (in addition to being a vocalist and a con artist, I'm an award-winning cake decorator) earlier today, Sylvester, aka the Snake, was fawning over Mother, as she twisted the curls at her nape and innocently batted her big cow eyes at him. Not yet fifty, she's a sharp-looking widow (for the second time), but too naïve to see what's going on right in front of her face. I'm the first to admit I'd said good riddance to my stepdad when the fat guy croaked a year ago, but Sylvester wasn't who I had in mind as a replacement. The idea of that viper-tongued thug jumping my lonely mother's bones makes my toenails waffle.

Razor stomps offstage. Since I still can't seem to summon my voice, Dougie finishes the song: "She disappears like smoke from a cherry bomb," and the Mercedes in my vision speeds off as smooth as a stealth jet into a starless sky. Disgruntled fans in the front row boo, and someone pelts me with a crushed cigarette pack. Dougie gets in my face, his eyes wild. "Hey, Jodie, what the fuck?" he whines, but I shove the cordless mic into his chest and run home, afraid for Mother.

I'm certain Sylvester is only after what (or who) my beer-barrel-gut stepdad cemented under the new patio a month before he was gunned down in a supposed carjacking; I say supposed because the crooks left the car behind. The only good thing about my stepdad being popped is at least he made Mother a very rich widow. In fact, she's astonished at how rich she is. It was clear to me that he was crotch deep in some shady deals because I'd been watching him for the Palizzi Brothers for years. What Mother doesn't know won't hurt her—let her think stepdad was a saint—but I can't bear to see Sylvester charm his way under her skirt, or under that patio. I have to save her. I know who's buried there, and she would be in a mighty tight spot indeed if she knew.

My heart starts jackhammering the moment I realize Sylvester's Mercedes is parked in her driveway. Hoping to catch him in a compromising position, I go around to the back of the house. As I near the sliding glass door, I hear a loud *pop-pop* that makes my stomach lurch up my throat. I'm too late, I think, as I force myself to look inside. I can't believe what I see: Mother is shaking her head as she stands over Sylvester, who's bleeding into the living room Berber. I bang on the glass, and she hurries to let me in.

"Where the hell did you get a gun?" I ask her. It looks like mine. In fact, it is mine. "Hey, why are you pointing it at me?"

"Get in. I don't know how to tell you this, sweetie, but it's time to enlarge the patio," she says.

Prepared
Sandra McDonald

1. For the Lights to Go Out

Massachusetts Hall was the oldest building on the Bowdoin College campus and damn drafty, too, especially on a February day that was colder than a witch's tit. Professor Ellie Comeau didn't normally think in terms of witches or tits but since moving to Maine she'd learned all sorts of local sayings about snow, sleet, and winter. Or maybe she was thinking about tits because the young student across from her, Tracy Gallagher, had shown up for her appointment in a very low-cut black sweater with a hint of black lace bra underneath.

Tracy didn't usually dress that way in class. Maybe she'd figured out that Ellie liked women and was hoping to distract her with firm, high breasts like pale melons.

"Tell me how you wrote your last essay," Ellie said, trying to keep her voice neutral.

An innocent, wide-eyed look. "I don't know what you mean, Professor. I just sat down and wrote my own thoughts."

"Your own thoughts are very similar to content available online," Ellie pointed out. "Word-for-word online, on Wikipedia."

The corner lamp brightened suddenly with a surge of power. Somewhere outside, an electrical transformer popped. The lamp and heater under Ellie's desk both died, leaving the office dim and her feet cold.

It wasn't the first time there'd been electrical difficulties, and goodness knew budget cuts kept the building unheated on weekends and holidays, but today the pop of the transformer sounded particularly ominous.

"Uh-oh," Tracy said.

"There's a generator," Ellie said.

The lamp and heater blinked back on. Almost immediately, however, they flicked off again. Ellie heard a distant humming.

Then more transformers popping, and the squeal of car brakes out on Bath Street, and the unmistakable crash of one or more cars.

Ellie moved to the window and pulled her gray cardigan tighter over her own breasts, which after fifty-two years of gravity were nowhere near as firm or enticing as Tracy's. Five years she'd been in Brunswick, you'd think she'd be acclimated, but usually the chill that settled into her bones by Halloween didn't dissipate until July 4th.

Another screech of brakes, another smash of metal on metal.

"I hope no one's hurt out there," Tracy said, but she didn't really mean it. She didn't care much about strangers. She did care about whether her boyfriend Rick Ney was in the library and not off with that slut Carrie Exling. The signal symbol on her phone was absent, though. No messages, no signal. "Should I come back tomorrow, when the power's on?"

Another transformer popped. Ellie imagined the whole town going dark, corner by corner—the downtown businesses and restaurants, the supermarkets and WalMart, the houses that stretched out along the peninsulas.

"All right," she said reluctantly. "I'll see you tomorrow."

After Tracy left, Ellie grabbed her own coat and scarf, locked her door, and followed the darkened stairs to the exit. Once outside, cold air slashed at her cheeks and nose. The accident on Bath Street was a big one—three cars wedged together, with a live electrical line snaked across one hood. Above their heads, several power lines sagged like wet clotheslines. Two transformers leaked smoke and red flames.

"Back up, people," a cop said. "Those lines snap, you'll be sorry."

Ellie told herself there was nothing she could do to help. She hurried toward Maine Street, her boots clicking on the shoveled pavement. Once she was away from campus, the overhead lines fell silent.

The side streets were empty, the houses still, and as the sirens rose in volume behind her she felt like she was the only person left in the world—isolated, cut off, about to meet a terrible end.

Five minutes later she let herself into her own house. A nice cheery fire was burning in the old fireplace. Dad was parked in his wheelchair beside it, staring gloomily at the flames.

"You know I hate these chemical logs," he said. "They smell awful."

He wasn't happy unless he had something to criticize—politics, her clothing, innocent Duraflame logs. She blamed the fact that he was alone all day, an old widower and his TV, no wife or love to call his own.

Ellie asked, "Did you eat lunch?"

"Tasted like cardboard."

"Any news?"

"Nothing but static."

Ellie got out their candles and flashlights, piled extra blankets on the sofa, and thought about sleeping arrangements if the power stayed off. When an oil lamp flared in Bob Cleaver's kitchen she traipsed across the snowy back yard and knocked on his back door.

He was ruddy and cheerful under a bulky red sweater. "Come on in. Hot chocolate? On the house."

"I don't want to leave Dad too long," she said. "Any word on how long it'll be out?"

He warmed his hands by the flames of his gas stove. "Not a word. Could have picked a better day for it, though. I had fifty students in the middle of an exam."

Ellie peeked into his living room. "No fire?"

"Chimney got blocked up over Christmas. I meant to have it fixed, but, you know. Better things to do."

"You should come over and sit by ours."

"Maybe later," he said, and watched her go back across the slippery yard. He didn't like Ellie's father. The old man sometimes had hookers over while Ellie was out—trampy women who showed up in skimpy skirts, their eyes as dead as lumps of dirty snow.

Bob wasn't opposed to pleasures of the flesh but he thought hookers were nothing more than disease-carriers, leaving god-knew-what kind of germs and bacteria in their wake. They were even worse than his students, who thought nothing of sneezing into their open hands and then handing in a paper or exam book with those moist, unwashed fingers and palms.

Bob washed his own hands five or six times an hour, depending on the circumstances. Which reminded him: the hot water would soon be out as the tank cooled. He should wash them while he could. And then boil some more water for use later.

You could never be too prepared when it came to germs.

2. For Emergencies Large and Small

Sixty-year-old Jack Rice had graduated from Bowdoin, taught politics at Bowdoin, and after a grueling year-long process of interviews and cocktail parties, had finally, *finally*, been appointed President of Bowdoin.

On good days he enjoyed wrangling over budgets and salaries. On bad days he was suddenly responsible for two thousand students and another thousand employees.

Today was a very bad day.

"We have generators," he reminded the people gathered in his office. "The generators have fuel. Why aren't they working?"

"Huge power surge through the grid," said Rob Parent, in charge of Facilities. "We used to have safeguards, but the upgrades last year came with faulty switches. We're fighting the manufacturer on that one, but they're fighting back. "

It was the kind of cock-up that might get Rice fired, even though he'd had nothing to do with it. He was going to have to shift blame to Parent, who he'd never liked much anyway—the man was a closet alcoholic, maybe even ran his own moonshine still in a campus basement somewhere.

"So because of some bad switches we suddenly have no heat in the cafeterias and thousands of kids who need dinner," Rice said. "What about the gas stoves?"

"Won't work. The computer controls are all down," said Lucy Gragert, the tall and beautiful woman who ran Dining Services. "We've got Sterno, but that's only going to go so far. Sandwiches, salads, lots of stuff we can serve up before it goes bad."

Rice tapped his pen on his blotter. It was a nice pen, heavy and black, good for signing his name in big flourishes. "No one can contact Central Maine Power. There's no radio or TV, no cell phones—" he turned to Mary Delgado, chair of the Physics and Astronomy Department. "Because of sunspots."

Mary Delgado suppressed a sigh. She knew she wasn't one of Rice's favorites, even though she'd won a Guggenheim Fellowship three years back and her work on compact binaries was earning recognition across the country. She was too short, too fat, and too ethnic for him. But she knew her sunspots.

"They showed up a few days ago, several of them, much bigger than expected at this time in the cycle—it was on the news, on the web," she said. She expected, and got, blank looks from everyone in the room. Nobody ever paid attention to science news except the scientists. "These were big enough to see without a telescope."

"If you looked straight at the sun and blinded yourself," Bob Parent joked.

Mary didn't tell him that you could look directly at the sun, under some circumstances, though you usually didn't want to. "Sunspots mean magnetic storms. Sometimes they fade away, and sometimes they flare up like volcanoes. Sometimes we get CMEs—coronal mass ejections. A billion tons of superheated plasma ejected into space at up to five million miles an hour. When a CME hits earth, it causes electromagnetic storms and we see aurorae like the Northern Lights. Or we can lose a power grid, like Quebec in 1989."

Rice stared at her. "So you're saying a volcano exploded on the sun and now it's our problem."

Mary thought he was being idiotic, but she kept her voice level. "I'm saying it's a distinct possibility. Or it could be a series of ejections. Sometimes CME's smash up against each other, like one ocean wave crashing into another. We call those cannibals and the power they can unleash—well, it's enormous."

"Wouldn't we have had a warning?" Lucy Gragert asked.

"Normally, it can take up to a day or more for a CME to hit Earth," Mary acknowledged. "But cannibals move a lot faster. If the military or NASA knew ahead of time, they didn't have time to tell the world."

"Maybe something blew up on the sun, and maybe it didn't," Bob Parent said, no amusement left on his face. "Whatever happened, we've got dorms full of freezing students and no way to get them heat."

Rice was thinking the exact same thing. He was also thinking about the campus Safety Department. Forty different preparedness plans and emergency procedures, everything from terrorist attacks and avian flu to safety policies for auditoriums, but not a single page about what to do with a prolonged power outage in the middle of winter.

Lucy Gragert said, "Most gas and oil furnaces won't work without electricity, but I've got a generator and fireplace at home. I can take students home with me. So can other staff and faculty. We could ask the townspeople to, as well. A lot of them have propane tanks and fireplaces. If we come together as a community, we can keep everyone warm and safe until the power's back on."

Rice wasn't much for the idea of letting a dozen college students into his house. And he definitely didn't like the weather forecast: deep-freeze tonight, high chances of snow tomorrow. He thought about his faculty, most of whom had gone home and couldn't be reached; about the Brunswick mayor and chief of police, who'd have their own hands full; about the likelihood that candles would cause fires in the dorms; the even larger likelihood that many students would try to drive home on bad roads and probably slide off into a snow bank and die, but the college would get sued because car accidents were somehow their fault.

For the first time since taking the job, he wished someone else were sitting in his chair.

3. For Predators

Tracy Gallagher was in her freezing cold dorm room, bundled up and sniffling, when her roommate Melanie Tyler came in and said, "I can't believe the generator's not on. Do they want us to die of hypothermia?"

Through tears, Tracy said, "I found Rick in Carrie's room. I hope they freeze in hell."

Back in September, Melanie had figured out that she and Tracy would never be lifelong friends.

Melanie was a solid, sensible girl from Hartford, Connecticut. Her parents sold insurance. She believed in hard work and keeping a 4.0 GPA, and she planned to lose her virginity only when she was good and ready. But Tracy—oh, Tracy. Her parents in Boston had money and so she had money. She'd never had a part-time job. She thought her college education should be seventy-five percent boyfriend and twenty-five percent showing up to class.

"Forget Rick." Melanie fished her favorite heavy socks from a drawer. "Let's go get dinner while there's a chance of getting something hot."

The line at Moulton Hall was out the door, with students shivering and complaining under the darkening sky. Thorne wasn't much better, with almost every seat already taken at long tables lit by candles and battery lamps. They had to sign in on a roster with their ID numbers because the cash registers weren't working. Melanie's hopes for hot food went unfulfilled but there were plenty of sandwiches.

"This is ridiculous," Tracy said, after they found seats. "I want to go home. I'm going to drive home."

"Don't be silly. What if you spin out? All the cell phones are out."

Tracy looked mulish. "I'm a good driver."

The students at their table had lots of theories about the power loss—terrorists, incompetence, freak storm upstate. Some had gone to WalMart to stock up on candles and chemical hand warmers but had to return empty-handed because the cashiers weren't taking credit or debit cards. There were a lot of jokes about sharing body warmth. Two campus employees appeared to announce that Smith Union would be open for the night, bring your own blanket; Melanie didn't see how it would be any warmer there than in her nice bed under a hundred layers of clothes and her down quilt.

"I'm going," Tracy said when they left the dining hall. "I can be home in two hours."

"Wait until tomorrow," Melanie urged. "It'll be safer in daylight."

"It's going to snow tomorrow. You want to come with me?"

Melanie shook her head. "I'll take my chances here."

Tracy left just before six o'clock. Melanie went down to the first-floor lounge and hung out with other girls until a terse security officer asked them to put out their candles and go to Smith Union. Melanie pretended to agree, but retreated to her room and read Moby Dick on her e-reader until the battery dropped to red. She was morally opposed to the slaughter of whales but an oil lamp would have been handy to have right about now, as would a bed warmer, hot water in the bathroom, and the prospect of hot tea in the morning. Surely the lights would be back on by then.

In the parking lot, Tracy saw a lot of empty spaces. The road was reasonably clear. But the corner of Maine and Bath was closed off, forcing a detour through side streets. Some people had fires going in barrels on their lawns, and a few houses had lights on thanks to generators. A long line of cars was backed up on U.S. 1.

Usually she'd get on her phone and talk or text until traffic cleared, but now there was nothing to do but listen to her MP3 player and curse the day that bastard Rick Ney had been born. When she finally got to 295 she saw Maine state troopers blocking the ramp.

"State of emergency," one told her when she rolled down her window to complain.

"This is an emergency," Tracy argued. "I'm trying to get home."

The trooper was unmoved. "Essential travel only. You have to turn back."

U.S. Route 1 to Freeport was blocked off as well. Tracy wasn't deterred.

She turned down winding, slippery Pleasant Hill Road and followed it to Freeport. A few other drivers had the same idea. The white dots of their headlights in her rearview mirror comforted her. The car thermometer registered 18 degrees and dropping outside, and the motels and restaurants she passed were all dark.

Just as she rolled into downtown, her gas light blinked on. The first gas station she saw was closed, as was the second.

She wanted to burst into tears all over again. Stupid car that needed stupid gas. But then she remembered that the L.L. Bean store was open twenty-four hours a day, year round, even on Christmas. She could go in, maybe sleep on the floor in a borrowed sleeping bag, and come morning the power would be back on and the gas stations open. She'd be in Boston by noon.

Tracy pulled into one of the enormous lots behind the store but kept the engine on. Everything else was dark—no moonlight or starlight, no streetlamps. Just the deep freezing cold and her own lights, spearing through the night and bouncing off snow piles.

Someone tapped on her window.

Startled, Tracy let out a yelp.

The man outside her passenger window wasn't much older than her, with parka hood framing his earnest, bearded face. She thumbed the button for the power window and cracked it open just two inches.

"Need help?" the man asked.

Tracy nodded. "Is the store open?"

"No. They closed an hour ago. First time in years. I work in the Security Department, just on my home."

"I'm trying to get to the highway, but I'm low on gas."

He looked thoughtful. "Well, there's no gas tonight. No electricity to run the pumps. And the National Guard's got the highway blocked."

Tracy could feel her eyes water. "I need gas," she repeated. "I can't get back to Bowdoin without it."

He hesitated. "We could siphon some from my truck, but I left it home. I only live a mile away. Can your car make it that far? You drive me home, we'll get you some gas."

Tracy hesitated.

She knew about predators. In tenth grade a wild-eyed man had grabbed her in the food court of Galleria Shopping Mall in Cambridge and tried to drag her out the door. This man was a lot more honest-looking, though, and after all, he worked for the store.

"Okay," she said. "Get in."

4. For the End of Us All

Keeping the fire burning all night for herself and her father used up three of Ellie's Duraflame logs. That left only two remaining. Six hours worth.

She walked back to campus in the freezing morning light—gray skies, snow on the way, the smell of ash on the wind—and got her car. WalMart was closed. "Cleared Out" said a big cardboard sign. She tried Hannaford and Market Basket. Lots of leftover Christmas decorations, but no logs or Sterno or flashlights. Two men in the parking lot at 7–Eleven were selling firewood out of the back of their pickup. Ellie spent all the cash she had, but it wasn't enough to fill the trunk.

She drove home and carried the wood into the house. It looked pitifully inadequate stacked next to the fireplace, and Dad said she'd paid too much. Ellie walked back to campus to get the flashlight she kept in her office. The department secretary Laura, an old crone who Ellie secretly called Battleaxe, was the only one in the building. She sat hunched behind her desk, layered in sweaters and scarves and a black hat.

"The school's asking faculty to take students in." Battleaxe's breath frosted in the air. "Sign up at Smith Union."

Ellie thought about her pantry. She'd taken inventory that morning. Between her and Dad, they had enough soup, vegetables and pasta for maybe a week. Not enough to feed refugees.

"They're sending food with them as well," Battleaxe said. "And spare furniture to burn, if you didn't stock up on wood."

"How long do they think this blackout's going to last?" Ellie asked, appalled.

Battleaxe coughed. She'd been feeling run-down for days, and was hoping that it wasn't that damn bronchitis again. Still, her medicine cabinet was full, as were her pantry and the woodpile. She always planned for bad winters. "Long enough. You prepared?"

"I'm fine," Ellie said.

Outside Smith Union, an enormous bonfire was burning on the lawn. The students gathered around it look tired from the cold night but also festive, too, with some battery-powered music and a snowball contest and free soda everywhere. Inside was crowded and chaotic but one of Ellie's students, Melanie Tyler, grabbed her arm and said, "Professor Comeau! Are you taking students home?"

"I don't know," Ellie said, looking for someone—anyone— who might be in charge. She saw the woman who ran the dining hall surrounded by an army of assistants, but not President Rice or his assistant deans.

"Take me," Melanie pleaded. "The dorms are freezing. I promise, you won't even notice I'm there."

Ellie liked Melanie—she came to class on time, did well on her papers, and acted like she really wanted to learn. But still. Refugees. Her hesitation must have shown on her face.

"You sign up over here," Melanie said, steering her toward sheets of paper on the wall. "We get a yellow form, and they'll give us food at Moulton. Thank you."

Soon Ellie had seven students signed out to her, including Melanie and another student from her class, Rick Ney. Ellie didn't like Rick much—he was too good-looking and he knew it. But he was also big and strong. Rick brought along a stick-thin brunette named Carrie, who was lugging a pillowcase of cosmetics and hair gels.

The other kids had blankets or pillows or backpacks jammed with sweaters and socks. Ellie led them home feeling like the Pied Piper with a ragtag band of coeds. Snow was beginning to fall, soft and fluffy and deadly.

"My father's kind of cranky," she warned before opening the front door. "Just be courteous, and it'll all be fine."

Dad was sprawled on the rug in front of the dwindling fire. Ellie stared at him, struck stupid. The wheelchair was upturned behind him. She thought maybe he'd tried to add more wood to the fire, or fix it to meet his own standards, and then overbalanced. Funny that he hadn't pulled himself up yet. Wasn't even trying.

Melanie moved forward first and dropped to her knees. Her finger went to Dad's neck. "No pulse. He's not breathing."

"Maybe we could do CPR," Rick said.

Melanie shook her head. Ellie wanted to slap her. If Rick wanted to try, then let him do it—let him transfer air from his young, strong body into the frail old thing on the floor, the thing that was her father, the man who had never stopped fighting since Vietnam.

"He's cold," Melanie said, and Ellie understood that cold meant dead, and dead meant she had to sit down before the room spun out beneath her.

"Sorry," Rick offered. A pitiful word, that, and he wouldn't meet her eyes. Instead he backed up against Carrie, who put her arms around his neck and buried her face in his chest as if she was the one who'd suffered the loss.

Melanie asked Rick and another boy to take the body into the dining room so the fire could be stoked up. They carried it out and another girl moved the wheelchair to the corner. The kids wrapped the corpse in pale blue sheets from the hall closet. Melanie gently said, "Professor Comeau, we don't know how long it'll be until we can contact emergencies services. We have to put him outside. Is there a garage?"

Ellie hadn't said anything during the wrapping. Words and articulation, her lifelong tools, had fled. But now she forced out, "There's a tool shed. I guess that will do."

Bob Cleaver was boiling water in his kitchen when he looked out his window and saw the somber procession. He came out to meet them and was surprised, if a little gratified, that Ellie sought out a hug. White snow drifted down on them, blanketing Ellie's hair and turning Bob's bare scalp cold.

"I wasn't here," Ellie murmured. "I shouldn't have left him."

Melanie worked on opening up the shed, whose door was wedged shut by snow. Rick stood with the body in his arms, his eyes focused on the nearby fence. Ellie was shaking against Bob's chest, but he couldn't lie and say he'd miss the old man. Instead he thought about the process of putrefaction, of how bacteria escaped from the intestines and started to eat its way through a corpse even in the cold. Rodents would sniff out the spoiling meat, even if it were frozen, and everyone knew that rodents were responsible for the Black Plague.

"Do you think that's the best place?" he asked, trying to sound sympathetic. "Maybe it would be more respectful to—I don't know. His own bed? Surrounded by his own things?"

Melanie yanked the shed door open. She knew Professor Cleaver only by sight. He was always carrying a canister of antibiotic wipes, as if he could disinfect the entire world. "He'll be fine out here."

Bob said, "No. It's not sanitary. You have to keep him inside."

Startled, Ellie pulled back from him. "Bob!"

"Take him inside," Bob insisted. "He can't be out here. Not with maggots and decay and he'll leak into the snow—"

They were all staring at him now. He could feel himself sweating despite the cold. He knew that look in their eyes. It was the look that his first wife had gotten whenever he started bleaching the bathroom at midnight, the look his second wife wore when he scrubbed his hands until they bled.

"It's not clean," Bob insisted, wishing they could understand, that they could see the world he saw, as the snow drifted down around them.

5. For More

Just before sunrise on the fourth morning of the blackout, Mary Delgado climbed up to the flat roof of her house and aimed her telescope east. She'd lost her solar filter over the years but it hadn't been hard to make a new one—cardboard, duct tape, some safety film she'd taken home from school. In the rooms below her feet, thirteen undergraduates were sleeping in heaps of blankets around the fireplace. The latest of Mary's refugees was Tracy Gallagher, brought back to campus by the state troopers after an assault in Freeport. The girl wasn't talking, but the bruises on her wrists and face told their own story.

At least she was alive, Mary thought. Hundreds of people in Brunswick weren't—people dead in house fires, or freezing in their homes, or in generator accidents, or dying from lack of medicine. Soon starvation would kick in, the canned food stretching only so far. The spring equinox was thirty-four days away, summer unimaginably further.

Still, Mary had hope. Sunspots came in cycles. A freakishly large CME was just that—an anomaly, unlikely to occur again. If she looked at the sun and it was clear, then she could hold out reasonable hope that the electrical grid would soon be restored and stay steady. If she looked at the sun and saw twisted, gnarled spots, then more devastation might be on the way.

The brilliant orb started up over the horizon. Mary hesitated. As long as she didn't look, she could imagine its surface clear and deceptively serene. As long as she didn't know for sure, she could dream of a restoration of normal life.

She prepared herself, and then she looked at the sun.

The Funhouse

Jessica de Koninck

Did you ever drive down Ocean Parkway
with the windows open on a summer
night and hear the fireworks even before
your dad parked the car and once

rode the horses at steeplechase and twice
went down the slide but did not dare
the parachute drop. In the dreamscape
the parachute never stops falling.

The rider always travels a little
too fast. Something's off kilter about
the man with the big teeth smile.
Something that says nothing

is quite right here, a horror movie,
never feeling fully awake. It's like that
when he places the coin in her mouth and
she begins to radiate and glow

like a painted wooden saint in one
of those old off the beaten track churches
where the artist didn't get the perspective
quite right, or maybe the colors, or the proportions.

You're not sure what, but the effect
is slightly askew, and that small misalignment
widens into the crack where fear enters
the room, rolls along the rotting slats

and hides with rats in broken eaves.
Remember getting lost at Coney Island.

As if in a dream the camp bus left. You stayed.
Your brother, bless him, cried until the bus

turned around, came back and got you,
both late for his birthday party,
your mother frantic. Now the Cyclone is dead,
the Ferris Wheel dismantled. No one screams.

No reason for fear, but when the man
places the coin in your mouth,
you turn into the light. The room
begins to spin. Everything disappears.

a c o r n s
Michael Kimball

Cast of Characters

TOM	30s-40s, An inventor
VAL	30s-40s, Married to Tom
BOY	Their son

PLACE:	A Hut
TIME:	Indeterminate

SETTING:	A lantern-lit room
AT CURTAIN:	Wearing something poor and rustic, Tom huddles over a table with a quill pen and several sheets of rough paper.

(The room is barren except for a propped up board for a table and 3 rough chairs. A kettle sits nearby, with 3 bowls. Burlap hangs over a window. By the number of papers strewn on the table and floor, we can tell that Tom has been drawing for hours, and it's clear that his imagination's on fire. He stops and studies his plans.)

TOM

No.

(He X's out a line and draws another line that curves carefully, carefully…)

(VAL crawls into the room from s.r. and stands, tiptoes over and kisses his head.)

VAL

I wondered.
(She goes to the window and pulls aside the blanket. The room brightens.)
It's gonna be a beautiful day.
(She studies him lovingly. He's oblivious to her presence, working feverishly.)
Want some tea?

(Tom squints at his work as if to ward off the distraction.)

VAL (Continued)

Hon? Want some tea?

TOM

Mm.

(Val smiles. Pours him a bowl of tea and brings it over. She studies his plans.)

VAL

Is that a torture rack?

(His trance broken, he looks up blankly.)

TOM

Hm?

VAL

It looks like a rack.

TOM

Rack? No.

VAL

What's that curvy little thing in his tongue?
(identifying other parts of the design)
I see the crank, the handle.

                           TOM
Hook. It's a hook.

                           VAL
Fishhook?

                           TOM
               (sipping the tea)
Mm-hm.

                           VAL
How about that long wavy line?

                           TOM
               (sighs)
Rope. It's rope. I'm really kind of busy here.

                           VAL
Is it upside-down?

               (He chuckles, giving up.)

                     VAL (Continued)
Well, I don't know.

                           TOM
He's hanging by his feet. With shackles.

                           VAL
Okay.

                           TOM
               (waiting)
Well—?

                           VAL
It's just—I don't know, shouldn't his penis be hanging upside down?

TOM

That's not important. Look. You turn the crank and the rope goes around here—See? I call it the Tongue-Stretcher.

(She stares.)

TOM (Continues)

It stretches the tongue.

VAL
(covering her letdown)
Oh! No, that's good! Really. I wondered what you were doing up so early.
(She goes back to the kettle and pours tea for herself, humming happily. Tom watches her. She looks back, sees him waiting.)
It's just so big. I didn't know if it might do anything else.

TOM

It's stretching the man's tongue! Automatically!

VAL

No, you're right.

TOM
(tossing his pen on the design)
I don't know why I bother.

VAL

Oh, I'm sorry, hon. Why don't you take a break, have some nice acorn soup. It's gonna be such a nice day.

TOM
(with a sigh)
Yeah. I suppose.
(getting up)
No! No. That's exactly why I bother. Acorn tea. Acorn soup. Because we're starving, that's why. And no one's got money to buy my butter churns.
(He sits back down.)

                              VAL

How far?

                              TOM

How far what?

                              VAL

—does it stretch?

                              TOM

His tongue? I don't know.
                    (measuring his own tongue)
Two inches? It depends how much you turn the crank. Three?

                              VAL

Okay.

                              TOM

Well, you can't stretch it too much, or he wouldn't be able to talk.
                    (beat)
Tell secrets?

                              VAL

Oh! You're so smart.

                    (He studies her.)

                              TOM

I was doing fine here. Fine. Without the criticism.

                              VAL

I'm sorry, I'm sorry—It's really—It's such a great idea.

                              TOM

It's a work in progress!

                              VAL

I know. I should leave you alone.

                    (From s.r. BOY crawls in.)

                         BOY
You guys. Do you have to make so much noise?

                         VAL
Oh, Daddy was working. I interrupted him. Want some nice
juice?
              (She fills a bowl from the kettle.)

                         BOY
Nah.
              (Boy heads to the table, looks at Tom's plans.)
What's that, a rack?

              (Tom keeps drawing.)

                         VAL
Is it a rack, he said.

                         TOM
I heard him.

                         VAL
              (to Boy)
It looked like a rack to me too. It's a tongue-stretcher.

              (Boy stares at the design, stares at Tom.)

                         TOM
Tell you what. Let's have breakfast.

                         BOY
Put it right-side up.

                         TOM
It is right-side up. He's hanging from— Okay. Here. Everyone
happy?
              *(Tom corrects the penis. He sees Val containing a
              laugh.)*

                         VAL
I'm sorry.

TOM
(good-naturedly)
Everyone's a critic.

BOY
What's that little thing in his tongue?

TOM
It's not little. A fish hook.

BOY
Where's the shackles for his wrists?

TOM
Why would he need—

BOY
To hold his arms down. You can't break him if he just hangs there, duh.

VAL
Boy, be nice.

TOM
I'm not finished. And it's not a rack. Can we eat?

BOY
Whatever. Mom, seen my rock?

VAL
Oh, was that yours? Tsk. I put it outside.

BOY
Mom—?

VAL
I didn't know.

(Boy crawls out s.l. Tom watches him.)

                              VAL (Continued)
Tom, he was only trying to help you.

                                   TOM
I know. I didn't get much sleep.

                         (Boy crawls back in with his rock and a handful of
                         acorns.)

                              TOM (Continued)
                         (to Boy)
Hey. Come here, take a look.

                         (Boy comes over. Tom dips his quill in the ink.)

                              TOM (Continued)
What do you think, big shackles? Little shackles?

                                   BOY
Hold this.
                         (Boy hands Tom his rock, sets his acorns down. Boy
                         takes Tom's quill and draws ropes from the man's
                         wrists to the bottom of the frame.)
So when you turn the crank, see? His whole body stretches.

                                   TOM
Probably need a bigger crank.

                                   BOY
No, just gear down. Dad—with pulleys.
                         (drawing)
One here. One here. See? Legs go up. Arms come down.

                                   TOM
That's a big stretch.

                                   BOY
Till the sockets pop.

                                   TOM
Ouch.

                          BOY
Keep crankin', and sooner or later, the arms or legs rip right off.
Usually the arms.

                          TOM
Arms because—?

                          BOY
They're skinnier. You never heard of the rack?

                          TOM
No, I know. But that's my point. The rack's been done. Tongue-
stretching, see, that's innovation.

                          BOY
Yeah. Also lame.

                          VAL
Boy, don't be fresh. Come on, men, clear the table for breakfast.
You don't eat, your guts are gonna shrivel up and spill out your
bottoms like old rope.

            (Boy stares at the drawing.)

                          BOY
Dad.

                          TOM
Take your rock, Boy.

                          BOY
Dad, no, listen. You could use the hook to pull his guts out.

                          VAL
That's an idea.

                          TOM
Well. Maybe a little over the top.

                        BOY
Whatever.

                        VAL
Tom—?

                        TOM
No, a little. I'm just saying, with the arms and, you know ...
there's going to be a little—well, a great deal of blood.

            (Dejected, Boy picks up his rock.)

                  TOM (Continued)
Then again, if there was an easy way to get at the guts.

                        VAL
Boy?

                        BOY
The bum. Obviously.

                        TOM
Bum ... Okay, and when you say "guts"—

                        BOY
Intes-tines. Pull 'em out his bum. See? Hook him back here.

                        VAL
Ooo. That would be a terrible thing to watch.

                        TOM
Val—? Men at work.

            (Val gathers the acorns and brings them to the kettle.)

                        BOY
Wait. He could watch! Aww, man! Look—
            (trying to take the quill, but Tom won't give it up.)

                    TOM
I got it, I got it—
                    *(But he doesn't get it. The quill sits poised in his
                    hand.)*
"Watch," you mean— With his eyes? While his intestines come
out?

                    BOY
Dad, give me the quill.
                    *(Boy trades him the rock for the quill—and starts
                    drawing.)*
See, you just move the crank here—and the pulleys here, here…

                    VAL
Boy, you are so smart. Isn't he?
                    (ladling out the soup)

                    BOY
See? So his neck snaps here—

                    TOM
                    (squirming, he can't look)
Uh-huh!

                    BOY
Keep cranking, then his back breaks down here, so he's turned
around—

                    TOM
Ho! Kay!

                    BOY
—Now he can see.

                    TOM
Ah. Time for breakfast, Mother?

                    VAL
                    (clearing the papers off the table)
My inventors.

> TOM
> *(hearing something)*

Shh.

> BOY

So, Dad, what do you think?

> TOM

Boy!

> VAL

Shh. Shh.
> *(They listen fearfully as an ARMADA OF HELICOPTERS comes out of the distance and flies overhead.)*

> BOY
> *(doesn't sweat it)*

They're Imperial.

> VAL

You sure?

> TOM
> *(with relief)*

Imperial.

> VAL
> *(bringing the soup)*

Here we go, nice and hot.

> TOM
> *(Tom takes a sip.)*

Mmm. Num-num.

> VAL

Tom, Boy asked you a question.

> TOM

Oh, yeah, no, sure. It's a good, um … No, you really gave me some great ideas there, Boy.

VAL

Oh, Tom.

TOM

I'm just saying, you start pulling intestines out, I mean, there's a lot of intestines. You just gonna let them pile up on the floor? See, you've got to think these things through.

VAL

Slow down, Boy. Don't stuff yourself, we don't want you choking.

(Boy slurps his soup—then pauses. Thinks.)

BOY

Dad… Dad…

VAL

Don't talk with your mouth full.

BOY

No, listen! We feed him his guts!

VAL

Boy, you are absolutely devilish.

TOM

What do you mean? You don't mean…

BOY

Yeah! While they're coming out, they're going back in!

TOM

Whoa. Uh-huh, uh-huh.

BOY

It works! Dad, look. Where's the—

(As Val has removed his drawings, Boy grabs a napkin and starts sketching on the napkin.)

                         BOY (Continued)
Look.

                         VAL
Boy, that's absolutely elegant.

                         TOM
Okay. Just—Devil's advocate. How's he supposed to talk? You
know, tell secrets?

                         BOY
Who cares? Are you serious? Who cares if he talks?

          (Tom studies the napkin. Val and Boy watch him.)

                         TOM
Well, I mean, isn't that the whole purpose here? Make him talk?

          (Boy smirks.)

                         BOY
Whatever.
          (getting up)

                         VAL
Tom—?

                         TOM
Boy? Did you finish your breakfast?

          (Boy lopes to the s.l. exit.)

                         BOY
Breakfast sucks.

                         TOM
          (standing)
Hey, hey— Hey! Watch your tone.

                         VAL
Oh, let him go.

(Boy crawls out. Val stands watching the exit.)

TOM

Kids. Jeez. They know everything.

VAL

I don't know. He's been so gloomy.

TOM

It's his age. He'll be fine.

VAL

I suppose. Maybe he's looking for approval. You know? He's not a baby anymore.

(Tom picks up the napkin, studies it. Val comes and stands behind him, makes affectionate contact.)

TOM

Huh.
(with pride)
It's good. It is good.

(She kisses his cheek.)

TOM (Continued)

Hm?

(She smiles, holding him.)

FADE LIGHTS. END.

SOS Written on the Back of a Zombie
Paul Kirsch

My name is Manuel. If you're reading this, you've killed one of them. Good for you. Don't waste time wondering how I got a naked zombie to lie still long enough to scribble a message on its chest. We'll get to that later. What's important is *why*.

For the record, I'm writing all over this dead gringo's body, using every inch of available skin as parchment. Except his head. You should have destroyed that part already. My brother Rico used to say I had brains. I hope I manage to keep them a while longer.

Go ahead and turn the zombie over to Side B. Start reading at the base of its neck. Don't worry about smudging. This is tattoo ink.

Now. Where to begin?

ONE

Ragged holes and powder burns marked where someone had emptied a clip into the old woman's chest. She continued to shamble down the middle of the intersection, bare feet dragging against hot pavement. *Abuela* had joined the ranks of the undead.

Campbell and I watched from the shaded awning of a pharmacy. I cradled an axe in both hands, the "break glass in case of emergency" kind. Campbell's aviator shades made twin mirrors of his eyes.

He nodded to the advancing figure, half a block down. "You see her, Manny? Mrs. Butterworth over there."

I'd smelled her first. One of the bullets must have ricocheted through her stomach like a pinball through a piñata.

"Si."

Campbell bit down on his toothpick, cracking it in half, and spat the shrapnel aside. "She's wearing a hospital gown."

I said, "Lots of shamblers came from the hospital. Bedridden folk in a public building? A free buffet for the walking dead. Let's put her down already."

Two months after the end of the world, I was amazed how easily that sentence came to my lips. The breakdown of death's barrier twisted the living as well as the dead.

I'd partnered on with Campbell after we met looting the same strip mall. He kept quiet at first. Decided what to make of our situation. I liked that about him.

Once he clued me in on his plan to survive, I liked him even more. A little ambition is good for the soul. Especially when you've been ratcheted down the food chain.

Apart from the axe, my possessions were limited to keepsakes from my brother's tattoo parlor: bottles of ink, Rico's battery-powered coil machine, and spare needles. The future would need an artist to commemorate the past. Flesh seemed an appropriate canvas.

"Hold a moment," said Campbell. He narrowed in on the dead woman. "The closest hospital is tens of miles away, and Marie Callender isn't winning any medals for the hundred-yard dash."

As if to prove his point, the *bruja* cracked her knees against the bumper of an overturned car. Even when their faces sloughed off and their eyes rolled like billiard balls, the undead lost all peripheral vision.

"So she's not one of the fast ones," I said. "Thank God." When Campbell didn't respond, I chewed over his meaning some more. "Okay. Distance. She's been dancing the zombie shuffle longer than most. What's that got to do with anything?"

"It has everything to do with everything," Campbell said. "You find investor zombies on Wall Street, and clown zombies in the circus. What's a *hospital gown zombie* doing this far from a hospital?"

Instead of waiting for a response, Campbell cupped a hand over his earbud radio. "Base is telling me to bring her in. Doc wants a closer look."

In the first weeks, survivor garrisons sprouted around the city like pimples. Internal strife and undead invasion popped them just as quickly. Most of the failed outposts scattered into fringe gangs. You've probably heard of the Remainders. If not, watch out. They were a bunch of spiritual nuts who turned into gun nuts when their God abandoned them.

Campbell said his compound was different. A holdout where everyone earned his place through community service. I had yet to see it for myself.

I said, "'Bring her in?' Are you insane? What does the compound want with some old lady zombie?"

"She's not just any old lady."

Campbell opened a black shopping bag decorated with red lips, and the words: *Double-Bagging It Since '69.* Once he found the necessary tools, he held them up to make sure I paid attention. His aviators reflected my unease: the face of a kid, barely twenty, with a pencil-thin mustache.

Campbell said, "This is a delicate operation, Manny. We have one chance to get it right." He glanced back to the dead woman, who flared her nostrils like a hound seeking our scent. "No weapons."

"I don't think I heard you right," I said.

"Catching one of *them* intact is a whole new order of complication," he said. "Let me explain how this is going to work."

When he finished, I started to shake with adrenaline. "Fuck me," I said. "My life used to be simple. You changed the rules."

Campbell said, "If there were rules to the zombie apocalypse, leave them in the box. Better not to know how easily the other side can win."

TWO

I should have ignored him and swung my axe into Dame Edna's brain. Things might have gone better that way, and you wouldn't be reading my story as it circles the drain of this dead zombie's asshole.

Campbell and I stepped into the street, leaving our weapons behind. He horseshoed around while I moved into the dead woman's field of vision.

"Hey, lady!" I said. "Your grandson's here to visit."

Eyes like flecks of dirty ice—she raised her chin to fix on me, baring rows of chipped and broken teeth. I'd never stood this close to one of them unarmed. My legs felt like string cheese.

Campbell crept from behind, slow and silent as a cat.

"You got any hard candy?" I asked. My voice cracked with a resurgence of puberty. "Got a dollar tucked away in your coin purse?"

She snarled and readied to lunge.

"Come take a bite, Golden Girl," I beckoned.

She started forward, a wrinkled cannonball of mouth and hair. Campbell struck faster. He grabbed her arms and yanked back, slapping a pair of handcuffs around her wrists in one fluid motion. She whirled to bite him. Campbell skipped away like a dancer.

One chance.

Miss Daisy's attention shifted from me to my partner. She wrenched her shoulders toward him, the cold fact of the cuffs unrealized. My heart vibrated like a cell phone. Campbell nodded to me as he backed away, maintaining the distraction. I breathed deep and readied my tool in both hands, the leather straps braced like a garrote.

When I stepped closer, the soles of my sneakers barely left the road. I froze.

Campbell said, "Do it now, Manny!"

Trying to mimic Campbell's fluidity, I looped the strap over granny's head, pulled back at the level of her mouth, and cinched the buckle at the base of her neck.

She made a gurgling protest and whirled to face me. A bright, red orb poked between her lips. I'd done it. Muzzled the rabid dog with man's best friend against zombie infection: a ball gag.

The old woman went nuts with primal disbelief. Campbell came up behind her in a battering ram tackle, sending her sprawling to the ground. She thrashed and bucked like a fish out of water. Campbell's boot pinned her to the spot.

"Score one for the living, bitch!" I shouted.

Campbell slipped off his baseball cap to smooth back his thinning hair. His hands trembled. "I hope we never have to do that again. Let's see what we caught." He hunkered down by her twitching legs. "Watch her mouth. I don't like surprises."

The dead woman strained with the effort to chew through the gag but her biting days were over.

Another toothpick appeared between Campbell's teeth. He gripped granny's ankles to steady her. Then he smiled, tugged at something and lifted it for me to see: a piece of paper dangling at the end of a string.

Her toe tag.

"Rebecca Squirm," he read. "Born 1937. Died two months ago. Complications after a blood transfusion." He pressed his earbud radio. "That does it. Time to head back to the compound. We've got her."

"*Who?*" I said.

He slipped the tag down his vest pocket. "The needle in the haystack. Midwife of the undead. Patient Zero. Our host monkey."

I blinked. "No shit?"

Campbell grinned. "No shit. The compound doctor enlisted a bunch of us to hunt down the first known infected: a dead woman who vanished from the morgue. He can use her to trace the chemistry of this thing. Find a vaccine. Maybe even a cure."

I released enough breath to fill a parade float, and slapped our trophy's flank. "Hear that, lady? You're gonna help us save the human race!"

A low growl built in granny's chest. Those dead, unblinking eyes narrowed on me.

Now you know why my story matters. Why I scribbled all over this undead carrier pigeon. But it's not finished. You could say it's just beginning.

Hate to say it, but this dead hombre is running out of space. I only hope that by the time I finish illustrating him I'll arrive at an ending I can live with. Or die with, as the case may be.

THREE

"Where exactly is this compound?" I asked.

We secured the last of Miss Havisham to a pushcart. The sex shop where Campbell looted his goods provided plenty of rope. Restraints intended to bind the living sufficed for the dead.

"It's a row of beach houses along Pacific Coast Highway," said Campbell. He kept to the head of our small caravan, his hand resting on a holstered Glock as if grateful to be there.

I continued to maneuver the cart around rubble and debris, wondering how we'd ever make it as far as PCH. Car pileups and freeway barriers made for endless, concrete canals packed with the ravenous undead.

"I know it sounds bad," Campbell said, "but the setup is legitimate. They stretched gangplanks between the roofs, so they can isolate any part of the compound at a moment's notice. Scrap metal welded to form an impenetrable palisade. The survivors can hold out, backs to the ocean, as long as they need to. It's the safest place left in all of California."

Campbell got a starry look when he spoke of the compound. The old lady was our ticket inside. Much to my relief, she gave up on struggling and stiffened like a mummy.

"Do they have seafood and beer?" I asked.

He smiled. "You know it, brother."

"Women?"

"The kind who used to say 'not if I was the last man on earth.'"

"Hell of a way to call their bluff."

Campbell laughed—a tired, deflated sound. "You've still got your needles? Once we arrive, I want a tattoo to commemorate this day."

I hefted my backpack. The jars of ink tapped around the small pocket. "It's a promise, amigo. I'll treat you like a strip of good vellum."

Campbell shifted from me to Mrs. Squirm. "How's our patient?"

"Not complaining."

He frowned and waved his fingers in front of her eyes.

"No response," he muttered. "Never seem them act this way. It's funny."

"How's that?"

Campbell shook his head. "I once read about a connection between our senses of taste and smell."

"Uh-huh."

"The human head is one giant nexus. Ear, nose, and throat. Think about it for a second. The undead aren't steady on their feet. We could attribute that to inner ear problems. Rotting in the summer heat, not to mention forgetting to blink, wreaks havoc on their eyesight. Yet they seem to have the advantage in one regard: *smell*.

"We've stumbled on something with this ball gag trick. We blocked off Mrs. Squirm's last sensory input. She's disabled. Neutralized. If we uncuffed her, she'd probably wander around like a lost child."

I wheeled Mrs. Squirm through a narrow channel of cars. "Yeah, that's great, *compadre*," I said. "Free-range zombie. Way to think like a survivor. If I came up with an idea that stupid, you'd leave me to the Remainders."

Campbell shrugged. "Just food for thought."

No sooner had he said it than an SUV lifted from the road, a cloud of flame blasting its undercarriage. The explosion seared my face and sent me flying back. I hit the edge of an open car door and went numb. The handcart collapsed nearby. Shrapnel and debris kicked upward, transforming my city into a war zone.

"God damn it!" Campbell said. "It's a trap!"

Bullet holes started to chip away at cars and pavement around us, tracing a path in our direction. Through the haze of billowing smoke, I made out the shape of Campbell plucking grenades from his belt and lobbing them into high windows.

Up in the surrounding offices, the Remainders wore prayer shawls, beads, headdresses and face coverings stitched together in a Frankensteinian amalgam of religion. The failure of their faith forced them to negotiate a different course toward immortality. Cleansing the world with fire.

Campbell tossed a second grenade, a third. They blasted windows apart and discharged the contents: bible pages, chakra crystals, red chunks of the living. The gunfire eventually stopped.

Through ringing ears, I heard his voice. "You okay, Manny?"

I pushed with my arms and tried to stand up. It didn't work. My legs wouldn't move. The car door must have hit exactly the wrong spot. Next to me, strapped down, the collapsed *bruja* narrowed her milky eyes, as if celebrating the culmination of her curse.

FOUR

Paralyzed. Game over. Dead end.

Campbell dragged me into the rubble of the nearest building, then gathered up the old witch. He positioned some desks and cubicle walls into a miniature barricade. I didn't like the way he walked. Hunched over, with an arm over his chest like a broken wing.

I said, "We're not gonna see PCH, are we?"

Campbell tapped his earbud. When his arm shifted, it made a wet sound pulling away from his bullet wound. He yanked the sheared radio wire from his vest, stared at it, and sighed.

"No, I suppose not."

"Neither will Mrs. Squirm," I said. "No more host monkey. No more vaccine."

Our cargo had resumed her unblinking, wordless vigil.

Campbell slumped down and considered for a long time. Then he muttered to himself: "One chance. We still have one chance." He smiled up at me. "Manny, I think I'm ready for that tattoo."

After digging through rubble to find my backpack, Campbell took out my brother's coil machine, spare needles, and plenty of ink. Then he explained how he wanted it done.

"I knew you were crazy," I told him, "but now you're actually insane. Not gonna happen, *compadre*."

Campbell said, "Look at my wounds, Manny. I'm a dead man. Least I can do is make something of the experience."

Without giving me a chance to fire back, Campbell removed Mrs. Squirm's ball gag. She blinked as her senses recalibrated, like a computer booting up. Campbell slipped his belt free and bit down on the leather.

"What the fuck are you doing?" I asked.

He closed his eyes and stuck his left hand by Mrs. Squirm's rotted mouth. When her teeth closed down, claiming two of his fingers, his grunt of pain vanished under the tide of my panicked screaming. Blood sprayed and bones crunched like twigs. The old woman yanked her head back and chewed at his offered flesh.

Trembling, sweating, and not bothering to staunch his wound, Campbell replaced her ball gag and stripped off his clothes. In another life, he could have featured on the cover of a romance novel. Now he was just a dead man, soon to be an undead man.

He took another pair of handcuffs from his shopping bag, and clicked his wrists behind his back.

"Better get started, Manny."

"*Jesus Christ!*" I said. "What's the matter with you? You want to be like *them*?"

He laid down in front of me and closed his eyes. "I wouldn't make it far with my wounds. I'll have a better chance of getting to the compound once I've changed."

"*Changed?*" I said. "What are you trying to—" Then the words went stale in my mouth. I remembered: *The tattoo needles.*

"You're an artist," Campbell said. "It's time to commemorate the day."

The pressure of tears welled up in my chest. I didn't let a single one fall. Campbell didn't deserve them. I could only help him die for the right reasons.

"You're a tricky bastard," I said. "Good luck."

"You too, Manny."

I slipped the toothpick from his mouth, popped in a ball gag, and tightened the strap behind his head. Then I filled the reservoir of my coil machine with ink, leaned over, and started to write it all down.

Campbell just stopped breathing.

EPILOGUE

If you're reading this, you've killed a zombie. Good for you.

I tattooed my location under his armpits, where rot and the elements won't diminish the ink. It's my hope that he'll meander, like a letter in a bottle, and eventually fall into the right hands. Yours.

Rebecca Squirm, the host monkey, continues to stare into space. Her lips are painted with Campbell's blood. Sometimes I wake up from fever dreams and catch her glaring at me. She's our last hope. Our last chance. And I'm starting to wonder how much pressure one ball gag can take.

Shit. He's waking up. Goodbye, Campbell. Goodbye.

If you're reading this, come find us.

Please.

In Security (Inanna Meets the TSA)
A.J. Luxton

She's flying home, at last, afterwards.

And they said, "Scuse me, miss,
we'd like to see that crown on your head,
too sharp, too precious, umm, no,
can't have it, would you like it mailed back to you?

and those rings in your ears, they have
powerful points, capable of violence."

"Gatekeeper," she said, "Why have you taken away
the beads around my neck?"

And, the underworld's keepers, they said,
"That's the way we do things around here."

"Gatekeeper, why have you taken away the toggle pins at my
breast?"

"Ma'am," said the Guardians, "it's just procedure."

and they strip-searched Inanna,
and took away the girdle of birth-stones at her waist,
because she could throw them and hurt someone, you know.
And they confiscated piercings,
underwire,
nail clippers,
boots,
memories,
subversive books,
time,

and she was late for her plane.

she got there just barely
in a flimsy hospital gown, running.
the cold touched her,
the flight attendants were nasty.

but when the wheels leave the ground,
she is moving forward,
again.

Anarchy Becomes Electra

Ellen Neuborne

By the time the sun was visible behind the line of blighted elms, Electra Mackey's team held the high ground of the battlefield. It had taken less than the allotted thirty minutes to initiate the sequence, move the civilians into a manageable herd, and line them up on the far side of the staging area.

Electra grinned at the speed with which the plan went down. She looked to the perimeter. Her advance scouts were in position. She was ready to give the order to move to Stage 2 when Corey Talisman, her latest recruit, began to cry that he was hungry for lunch.

The whining went like a chain reaction through the team and it was only moments before they were all back at Stage 1: the rank and file of Miss Heather's pre-K class. Electra slumped helplessly against the monkey bars as the willowy 20-something swooped in to retake control of the dozen four-year-olds.

"Lunchtime, lunchtime, line up for lunchtime," she sang.

"Coming Electra?" Miss Heather's voice sounded wobbly, but bold, as though she'd just learned there were no monsters under the bed after all. "Yes, Miss Heather," said Electra, tugging at her starched white collar. She got into line, size order behind Aldo Boniface and in front of Grace Lee.

Miss Heather took her position by the door of the fenced playground and raised her hand. "All together now," she ordered.

The class chanted in unison:

My hands are at my side
I'm standing straight and tall
My eyes are looking straight ahead
I'm ready for the hall.

Miss Heather held the door as her class marched past her and into the hall of Fiat Lux Academy, merging with the mass of children headed for the cafeteria. She kept smiling, but averted her eyes as Electra Mackey passed by.

Electra followed her classmates. She clapped in time. Her chant under her breath was barely audible.

It had been six months since Electra and her classmates joined the ranks of the educational lottery winners and entered the halls of Fiat Lux, New York City's premiere pre-school prep school. Ever since New York had attempted to egalitarianize the educational system by making all schools public and all entry by intellectual merit alone, families had stopped trying to buy their way into elite schools and turned their efforts toward the one and only portal: the workings of the four-year-old mind. New York's children were judged on just one exam—the Standardized Measurement Assessment and Ranking Test (or SMART) given at the end of a child's fourth year on the planet. That score, and that score alone, determined entry into the city's stratified academies. And once inside, there was little room for maneuvering. The SMART became more than a test: it was a life sentence.

Not surprisingly, New York soon found a way to monetize the trend. For-profit test preparation schools popped up all over Gotham's map. Each more rigorous than the next, they promised the petrified parents top-performing tots in exchange for top dollar. Nicole and Mark Mackey had refinanced their junior classic six at wildly unfavorable terms to raise the necessary cash to pay off the administration and get Electra in the door at Fiat Lux.

"Just don't call it a cram school," said Nicole, as she sewed the last of the gray and gold patches onto the six size 4T blue blazers.

"Why not?" Mark wanted to know.

"It makes us seem desperate."

"Aren't we?"

Nicole didn't bother to answer her husband. She gathered great handfuls of her daughter's long brown curls and pulled her tiny face in for a kiss.

"Who is Mommy's little genius?" she asked.

"I am," giggled Electra.

The Fiat Lux curriculum was based on the theory of intensive instruction, followed by recitation—known in the faculty lounge as Drill and Drone. Teachers packaged reams of knowledge in mathematics, physical science, and philosophy into an onslaught of catchy chants and songs.

The product of fractions is plain to see
When you learn this algorithm, sing it with me—
(A over B) times (C over D) equals
(A times C) over (B times D)—
See, it's easy as easy can be
Sing it once again now, one, two, three.

They marched their tiny pupils through the material, doling out bite-sized bits of Power Bars and Red Bull–spiked apple juice as rewards. Still, one third of the students washed out in the first month. Their school IDs were taped to the wall outside the janitor's closet with red Ghostbuster lines slashed across them. Electra avoiding looking at the pictures as she passed by, keeping her gaze fixed on the double-high frosted windows that lined the halls and school cafeteria. On the other side, she could make out the tower of Lower Oracle, New York's top-ranked elementary school, across the street. It loomed tall and vague on the other side of the cloudy glass.

Work continued apace at night, when Fiat Lux students were expected to devote three hours to "home enrichment" via the school's web-based instruction manual. Among the parents, it was known (but never discussed aloud) that headmaster Francis K. DePlano had adapted (stolen?) the curriculum (strategies?) from the educational materials of his previous employer, the IRS (CIA?). As a result, it was heavy on math, science, and engineering and light on art and poetry.

"Which is fine, because poetry got me nothing but a dead end," said Mark Mackey, a digital advertising copywriter and veteran of four companies, two startups, and three rounds of layoffs. "All I know how to do is beg for my job in iambic pentameter. But not you, princess," he said, pointing his spoon at his daughter across the dinner table. "You'll have skills."

Electra smiled and swallowed to force the mouthful of macaroni and cheese down her throat. She liked it better when her father ignored her and just ranted about the cost of living.

It was in January when Mark came home late and got to the table when dinner was half finished. Nicole began to scold him with statistics about absent parents and educational performance but he waved her off. "Seriously, Nic, not tonight. Word is there's another round of layoffs brewing and I'm not sure how I stay out of sight this time. The axe is swinging in all directions."

"You're a key driver of profitability. You'll be fine."

"I don't know. Rick Parness got walking papers last week and his division hit all its targets last year. There's no metric for job security."

"I'm sure—"

"You have to stop saying that." Mark sat down at the table with a thud. "There is no 'sure' any more. There's just 'winner' and 'loser.' And this is not a good month for us to have that contest."

"We could talk to the bank."

"And tell them what? That we want out of the contract we signed last summer promising to pay 5% until the new year and then swallowing whatever the new rate might be? 'Cause that's going to be fourteen-fucking percent, Nicole. And that takes our monthly to what? I don't even know."

"Four thousand, seven hundred one dollars and twenty-two cents," said Electra miserably.

Nicole and Mark turned to look at their four-year-old, who had pushed her plate of Hamburger Helper back and was scribbling quickly on her dry-erase Math Meals placemat. The white shiny rectangle trimmed with smiling integers was filled with blue equations in Electra's neat crayon scrawl.

After a long moment, Nicole scraped back her chair and began wordlessly to clear the table.

When the apartment was dark and the sound of her father's shouting had faded, Electra got up out of bed and restarted the computer on her Disney princess desk.

While she waited for it to boot up, she fussed with the one toy still outside the confines of her always-closed toy box: a beach scene snow globe purchased the previous year on the family's one-week Jersey shore vacation.

Electra liked to shake the orb and watch the shells, sand toys, and beach-going family swirl around. She kept her eyes on the people, watching them soar up into anarchy, spin dizzily in the sandstorm, and then land, every time, on their feet, smiling, steady, together again. Shake, spin, settle. Shake, spin, settle. And if by chance a mishap occurred and a bucket landed on a head or a fish out of water, no matter. Electra just shook once more and then waited for all to be right again.

When the monitor sprang to life, she placed the globe by the mouse pad and opened the Fiat home enrichment program. As the sands settled, she began clicking along the icons on the left-hand side of the page.

"What kind of cookies do you think we'll get today?"

Miss Heather addressed her class in her singsong soprano. Every day, Fiat's sullen front desk matron delivered cookies to each classroom. Each day, a different kind.

The eager hands shot into the air.

"Oatmeal!"

"Sugar!"

"Chocolate chip!"

"It's graham cracker," said Electra, not bothering to raise her hand.

Miss Heather looked her way. "You sound pretty certain, Electra."

"I'm right," Electra replied.

And she was. That day. And the next. In fact, Electra was right every day that week.

During afternoon calisthenics, Electra explained it to Simon Oliver, who was doing jumping jacks beside her. "It's called probability. It's on the home enrichment site if you click ahead a little. Know the puzzle pieces, solve the puzzle. How many days do we get cookies? How many kinds of cookies are there? How often do those cookie flavors come? When you know the pieces, you can put them all together and it tells you what cookies are probably coming."

"So you're not reading Mrs. Walsh's mind?"

"Who?"

"The cookie lady."

"Nope. No mind reading. Just math."

"Cool."

"I guess."

"Well, it scares the beans out of Miss Heather."

"Yeah," said Electra, touching her toes and smiling. "It freaks her out."

Simon spread the word of Electra's discovery and soon Miss Heather's students—drilled to the hilt in applied mathematics and situational problem solving—were taking home enrichment time to new levels. At first, it was just a tool to predict what foods were being served—When was taco day? How long 'til apple-grape juice boxes? But then, energized by their newfound power to unnerve Miss Heather, they branched out.

Orren Moshmann counted footsteps and mapped travel patterns in and out of the classroom. Then he marshaled Julia P. and Julia M. to help him move the blond wood cubes that made up the classroom furniture. With the new floor plan, the class was able to line up in record time that afternoon, achieving the goal of a promised pizza party—a target they had not come even close to for months. The class cheered wildly as they marched into the hall. Miss Heather frowned but said nothing.

Corey Talisman found a section of the website that dealt entirely in electronics. Using safety scissors and Mrs. Walsh's crochet needles, he rewired the classroom light circuits so that they flashed in random sequence. The children seemed not to notice. Miss Heather developed a twitch by her left eye.

Kelsey Schiff discovered a way to predict who Miss Heather would call on to stand and recite at morning meeting. The combination of the class list, days of the week, and the number of times Miss Heather made eye contact with a particular student in the preceding afternoon helped Kelsey come up with the formula. After a week of study, she could narrow it down to three possible students—allowing the rest a night off to watch *SpongeBob SquarePants* on YouTube. Realizing that somehow she was giving herself away, Miss Heather stopped looking at her charges entirely, teaching to the air above their heads.

Meanwhile, Electra moved from math to logistics. She turned the pre-lunch playground period into her own personal human behavior stage, finding ways to move the children around in patterns, looking for ways to predict where and how each would turn. She honed her skills, watching, then closing her eyes, practicing her craft. "Grace is on the slide. Julia P. is behind me. Simon is by the sandbox." Her accuracy was so good, soon her classmates refused to place bets. "No fun when you're always right," groused Aldo.

"Sez you," Electra responded.

It was almost Valentine's Day when Electra, the Julias, and Sloane Miller began tracking the comings and goings of Miss Heather's Wall Street boyfriend Damon from his pickup spot in front of the school. Calculating the number of days he came and the number of minutes he was late and factoring in his age, they came up with a probable outcome.

Julia M. broke the bad news to Miss Heather. "He's going to dump you."

"What?"

"On or about March 17. Sorry."

When March 15 came and Damon didn't show up outside the school, Miss Heather quit. She left the school, her apartment, and New York City. "Like she was running from something," said Mrs. Walsh conspiratorially.

The office sent Mrs. Killinger to take over. Electra reported the teacher-switch that night at dinner. "That's nice, sweetie," said Nicole absently. It was just Electra and her mother at the table these days, now that her newly laid-off father had taken to spending his days at the retraining center. And nights at the corner bar.

Electra resolved to make her move.

"We should do it now," she told Simon.

"Do what?"

"Take the school."

"What?"

"It's better than standing around, waiting for whatever's going to happen," she said.

Simon thought about it while he munched his cookie. Then he nodded.

It took eight weeks of drills to get Electra's dozen to respond to commands. By May, she could maneuver them effortlessly through the playground. Then she moved on to other places. Calculating the position of hall monitors, she moved teams through the corridors, up the staircases, in and out of the administration offices, all undetected. Finally, in one glorious foray, she sent a duo to the corner for candy. When Grace Lee and Samuel Harris appeared in the classroom, fistfuls of red licorice in hand, Electra knew they were ready. "Tomorrow," she told them. "Tomorrow, we take it all."

The next morning, Mrs. Killinger's class was oddly quiet. No one called out. No one pulled hair or pushed in the hall. The class seemed unnaturally placid, like a waveless sea. Mrs. Killinger didn't think too hard about it. In fact, she didn't do much thinking at all. She was mere months from Social Security and not much interested in what would happen to the screechy little munchkins once she walked out the door. After recess, in which she absently watched them play that line-up-and-march game for the hundredth time, she called them to order and headed them off toward the cafeteria.

Electra felt like her heart was pounding in her mouth. She waved Team 1 into position. Corey and Julia P. sprinted ahead, jamming chairs under the knobs of the far doors. Team 2 did the same to the other set after the class had entered. Aldo walked alone though the single swinging door that hid the kitchen. There, four food service workers wearing starched white chef aprons and hairnets were scrubbing pots.

"Run," he said to them in Spanish. "It's all over but the killing." Looking at the little boy in a blue blazer wielding a serrated steak knife, all four workers sprinted out the back door to the street. Aldo propped a plastic milk crate up beside it, hopped on, and slid the deadbolt shut.

"Clear!" he yelled.

Back in the cafeteria, Electra and the rest of the children had pinned Mrs. Killinger, backing her into the corner and toppling the tables to block her exit. She stood trembling, her back against the wall of frosted glass.

The lunch monitors, caught off guard on the wrong side of the doors, were pounding and hollering. "What's going on in there? Open this door! What's going on in there?"

Electra, holding one of the knives Aldo was distributing around the room, climbed on top of the upended table and pointed to Mrs. Killinger. "Tell them," she ordered.

Mrs. Killinger began to scream. "Help! Help! The little buggers have gone mad!"

"What? What's going in there? Irene? Is that you? Open the door!" It was Mrs. Walsh.

"Help!" yelled Mrs. Killinger again. "They've got weapons!"

The banging on the door continued. Electra turned to Samuel. "Now," she said.

He hopped down from the table and raced to the far end of the cafeteria. There he, Aldo, and the Julias began stacking chairs. The ladder grew higher and higher, until finally, the last chair was used and Samuel turned back to the crowd. "Ready for Corey!" he yelled.

Corey stepped forward, tools in hand—a bottle opener, a corkscrew, and a butter knife. He began to scale the tower.

Electra shook with excitement. At the top of the ladder was the PA system. Once inside, Corey would hack the wiring and she'd be able to address the whole school—110 four-year-olds all over the building. She'd been practicing her speech all week.

"Is this fun? No. Is this what we want? No. Is this what we have to do? No! We are not responsible for how unhappy our parents have become. It's not our fault they're miserable. It's not our fault they can't make enough money to survive. It's not our fault that they hate themselves. We didn't do it. We won't serve time for it. We say no. We say no. We say no, no, no!"

"Oh, no."

The speaker was Orren Moshmann. He looked totally miserable. Electra followed his gaze to the top of the chair tower. There was Corey, on top of every single chair in the room, one foot short of the PA system.

"Can you jump?" called Sloane.

"That won't matter. He can't jump and do the wiring at the same time," said Grace.

"Can we get another chair?"

"From where?"

"What about a table?"

"Can't put a table on top. You'd have to take the whole stack down and start over."

Electra looked at the frosted glass walls and saw half a dozen fuzzy red lights flashing on the other side. "No time," she yelled.

Julia M. and Aldo began to climb up the tower. "We'll boost you up, Corey," called Julia as they rose.

Seeing the police lights at the window gave Mrs. Killinger new life. She took off her shoes and aimed them at her tiny guards. "Mealy mouthed rug rats!" she shouted, clocking Kelsey across the temple. "Insufferable little brats!" She pushed the table back against the three tiny soldiers on the other side.

At the far exit, the first boom shook the doorframe. "Battering ram," said Simon. He'd climbed up on the table beside Electra. He looked at her. "They'll be in here in a second."

Electra jumped down. She ran to the center of the room, a knife in each hand. The far doors shook with each pounding. The near doors began to rattle as the police worked that one, too. Electra stole another look at Corey. He continued to hop uselessly at the top of his tower, tall—taller than he'd ever been—and yet not tall enough.

The far door cracked open. Electra sat down on the floor. Mrs. Killinger ran in her direction. Electra nodded and dropped her head to her hands. The doors burst inward. Electra began to cry.

Her first cries were soft, but quickly she was wailing. As if contagious, the whimpering spread. In less than 30 seconds the children dropped the weapons and their bravado and became a sniveling, sniffling mass of sobs.

Electra kept her head down and watched as her tears splashed down onto the faux marble linoleum. She felt a big hand pat her head. "It's okay, dear. Let's just get ourselves together, shall we?" It was Mrs. Killinger.

The "unpleasantness" in the cafeteria was communicated to the parents via a brief email. No mention was made of weapons or police or battering rams. Mr. DePlano was able to keep it all quiet by promising admission of the children of all the responding officers. As a result, the official paperwork recorded the event as a food fight.

Mrs. Killinger retired early, her students distributed among the other classes at Fiat. All except Electra. Declared "above and beyond the curriculum" she finished out her pre-school year on the computer, at home.

The September air still felt summery. Electra stood on the asphalt yard of Oracle. Having aced the SMART, she was poised to start her kindergarten year. She hiked her knee socks up and looked around. Adults and children swirled around her. Electra squinted in the sun and tried to get her bearings.

"Hi, Electra."

She turned around. It was Simon. And Corey. And Julia M. And a new kid Electra didn't recognize.

"This is Bob."

"Seriously?"

"My parents say my name gives me an air of traditionalism."

Electra shrugged.

"We think Bob is kind of cool," said Julia.

Electra gave him a second look. Bob had coarse blond hair. He was pale—which made his brown eyes seem extra dark. He had long skinny limbs and his wrists stuck out from the edges of his maroon Oracle blazer. And he was tall. At least a head taller than any other kindergartener on the yard.

"He's got reach, too," said Simon. "Show her, Bob." And Bob reached up into the sky.

"Impressive," said Electra. "Welcome to the club, Bob."

"Thanks."

Electra surveyed her team. "Ready?" Nods all around.

The five linked arms and moved forward, in the direction of Oracle's lone security guard.

Android Growth Process

A.J. Luxton

She is listening to tapes to learn how to be human.

The tapes have language, and she
has language now: delightful! Watch her monologues.
You've never heard
such confidence, on stage, in life. This young one
is so happy.

No, I know she doesn't see you;
it's normal, that comes later. Yes, she'll say hello
but don't expect she'll feel your cues yet,
don't expect she'll parse. A young one.
She still feels like steel now; still can hear, in the dark,
the whirring of her metal heart.

You'd think she'd be anxious, wouldn't you?
I tell you—she has no fear. That comes later.
She won't learn how to be afraid
until the human language drowns out her metal heart,
leaving only the sound of not knowing what to say.

Qin and Snake
Karen Bovenmyer

Morning was very cold and very bright on the prairie. All around her, Qin's cousins blinked their black eyes in the glare, their furry bodies trembling. They were afraid.

Not Qin. She liked everything new, even sunlight, even cold. She tucked her stubby black-tipped tail under her and rocked, holding her hind paws. The morning smelled new, frost and dew melted together, air blew and ruffled her fur, and it was nothing like the boring nursery chamber at all. She could hear her uncles and aunties as they stretched and chirped the "all clear" around her. She hopped out into the prairie to look for sweet blue grass.

"Qin! Don't go too far from the burrow. Stay where Auntie can see you." Auntie groomed Qin's ear. Qin didn't like it when she did that but held still and let her. She knew it was important to let the adults have their way, or she would be sent back into the burrow. "You must stay where we can see you. There are hawks, foxes, and snakes who would make a quick meal of a prairie dog pup. They aren't like us. They can't talk and they don't have feelings."

"Yes, Auntie. I won't, Auntie," but Qin was already hopping away. She found some wide grass that was fresh and cool in her mouth. Then she found a bright yellow flower nodding in the wind—it left yellow dust on her paws when she caught it and made her sneeze. Next she found a pretty green and blue fly with delicate shimmering wings. It flew away when she tried to groom it, so she hopped after it. Soon she was in a place where the prairie grass blew tall around her and she couldn't see anyone.

The fly landed on a speckled stone and Qin crouched down on all fours and moved slowly through the grass. Just before she pounced the stone moved and the fly flew away. Qin had never seen a stone move by itself before. It slipped away from her like Auntie's tail when she was playing chase. She followed after the stone, scampering ahead to see where it was going. It got bigger and bigger until it was almost as thick as she was, and it wove around the grasses like a long, long tunnel through the burrow. Finally it ended in a knob. The stone had eyes.

"Good morning," it said, the long tube of its body coiling and uncoiling.

Qin was so surprised she almost stood up on her hind legs and chirped before she remembered that she didn't want Auntie to see how far away she was from the burrow. She ducked instead.

"What burrow are you from?" she asked. Its eyes were amber with black slits striping down the middle. She had never seen anyone who looked like this before. She had never met anyone so beautiful.

"Over there." It lifted its tail, a series of stones piled on top of each other smaller and smaller. Qin decided it was a young boy stone; his slow voice whispered when he spoke, and he groomed the air in front of him with a black forked tongue.

"I'm Qin!" She stepped forward and ducked under his head, grooming his neck in greeting. The great column of his neck pulled away from her and he studied her with his amber eyes. When she tried to lick him again, he held still. He tasted like grass that got too wet in winter. There was a strong smell she'd never sniffed before that made the fur stand up on the back of her neck. It wasn't pleasant, but it was new and different. She felt his tongue flicking through the fur between her ears. "I'm from over there." She pointed toward the burrow.

"We can't be friends," he said and slithered away from her. The stone had no legs, and watching him move was like watching water flow.

Qin frowned and her whiskers twitched. "Why not?"

"I'm a snake."

Qin stood straight up and chirped in alarm. Snakes ate prairie dogs! He flowed through the grasses away from her. She watched him find his burrow, it wasn't far, and he slithered away inside. She was still standing and chirping when Auntie and Uncle and several cousins came to see what the fuss was about.

Auntie smelled Qin and stood on her hind legs and chirped, short quick barks. Uncle smelled Qin and stood high and chirped. Her older cousins did it too.

"Snake snake snake snake," the chirp warned. Another Auntie and Uncle came over to check, and there was a great deal more chirping and general ruckus.

"Where is it?" Auntie said, after she had calmed down.

"He's gone," Qin said, thinking about the way his scales had shone in the sunlight, and how lovely he'd been when he moved through the grass.

"Don't ever go so far away from the burrow," Auntie said and nervously groomed her paws. "You come back right now and go inside." Auntie nipped Qin's heels all the way back home.

Everyone was very upset that night. The Aunties and Uncles talked for a long time. Snakes did not belong here! Snakes were dangerous!

Qin listened to everyone, but she knew better than to tell Auntie the snake could talk. Auntie was very firm that it was wrong to make up lies, and lies were whatever Auntie didn't believe.

Qin wasn't allowed to go out for several days, and neither were the other pups. Everyone was very worried, but nothing happened. Finally all the Aunties and Uncles got tired of tripping over pups and smelling the stale air down in the tunnels. After some very close watching for the snake, everyone was allowed to go outside again.

The sunshine was bright and the wind was fresh, and an Uncle from another burrow was visiting so Auntie was very distracted. Qin pretended to look for grass. She pretended to bat at the nodding flowers (though she really did sneeze from the yellow dust), and finally ducked low in the tall grass.

She found him on a flat rock, his coils wrapped all around him. He glimmered in the sunlight.

"Hello." Qin hopped over.

The snake lifted his head, but then turned away. "Oh, it's you. I told you, we can't be friends."

"Why not?" Qin wrung her paws together. He was much more interesting than anyone in her burrow.

"I'm a snake." He hissed, as though that were all the answer she should need.

Qin remembered the warnings about snakes being dangerous, but her snake didn't seem threatening at all.

"What are you doing?"

"I'm taking in the sun."

Qin sat next to him and took in the sun too. It was warm across her head and back, legs and paws. She could feel the cold rock underneath them.

"Don't you get too hot?"

"That takes a long time," he said. He didn't speak again and Qin was happy he didn't tell her to leave. She petted his scales with her paws. He was still cool. She leaned against him. After a long while his coils wrapped around her.

"You're warm." He said. He put his head in her lap and she heard his breath whistle. Big drops of water welled up under his pretty amber eyes.

"What's wrong?" Qin groomed his head.

"I'm lonely."

"Not anymore," Qin said and she hugged his cool head.

They talked in the sun for a long time, until they got too hot so they played in the cool grass. She loved to watch him weave through the prairie. He rattled his tail for her. He showed her what his scales looked like on the underside. She showed him how she could pick things up with her paws. She showed him how to roll in the grass to get rid of itchy spots. They chased some flies together and he ate one. She told him all about the burrow and her whole big family. He told her he was born with many brothers and sisters, but they all went to different places right away and he never saw them. He was alone all the time.

Qin thought this was very sad. She sometimes got tired of all her cousins and aunties and uncles but she loved them very much.

"You don't have to worry about that," she said, "now that we're friends."

"I wish that were true," Snake looked back at his burrow. "You know we can't be." Qin didn't understand why he kept saying that. Of course, she knew Auntie wouldn't approve of being friends with a snake, but Auntie didn't need to know, did she?

They sat together in the light until the sun dipped over the green edge of the prairie. The ground cooled and Snake became slow and languid again and curled around her for warmth.

Qin woke because she heard her name. She'd been dozing in Snake's coils.

"Qin! Qin! Where are you?"

Aunties and Uncles! She pushed at Snake, but he was cold and slow to wake.

"Qin!" Auntie rushed through the grass and saw Qin and Snake. She rose on her hind legs and chirped. "Danger! Snake! Snake!"

Uncle came through the grass and chirped too.

"It's okay! He's not dangerous!" Qin squeaked, but nobody was listening to her. They chirped and they hopped. Uncle darted close and nipped at Snake. Snake coiled in on himself and shook his rattle. Auntie nipped from the other side. Snake shook his rattle at her, too.

"Stop! He's my friend!" Qin said, but no one could hear her over the danger chirps. The visiting uncles came, and more cousins, and many more adults until Qin could barely see Snake. They dove at him and nipped. He tried to strike back and missed because the chill made him sluggish.

They nipped at him until he managed to slither safely back into his burrow. Qin breathed a sigh of relief. But Auntie was still chirping. Uncle turned around in front of Snake's burrow and kicked dirt into it, covering his shining scales. They would bury Snake alive!

"Stop! Stop!" Qin cried but no one listened to her. She clung to Auntie and tugged on her paws.

"It's all right," Auntie said when Snake's burrow was nothing but a misshapen pile of dirt. "The bad snake is gone." But Qin was crying too hard to listen.

After everyone groomed the snake smell off of her, Qin was punished for running away. She had to bring everyone else sweet grasses while they all talked about what happened. Every pup was told over and over not to go away from the burrow. The adults told many stories about how snakes killed and ate prairie dogs. Qin plugged her ears.

Finally everyone went to bed, curled in and among each other to share warmth. Qin thought about poor Snake and what happened.

"Don't cry," Auntie patted her on the back. "It's all over now."

"Poor Snake," Qin finally managed to say. "He was my friend!"

Auntie was quiet for a long time.

"Qin," she said, patting down Qin's fur between her ears. "That snake was not your friend."

"But he didn't try to eat me. He was just lonely."

"I told you. Snakes don't have feelings. It probably wasn't hungry, little pup."

Qin shook her head and Auntie sighed.

"What do you think happened to your mother?"

Qin sniffled. She still missed her mother. "What?"

"She was eaten by a snake. They only eat sometimes, and that sometimes lasts them a long, long while."

Qin thought about that long after Auntie went to sleep. Snake was her friend. She knew he didn't eat her mother. She knew he would never eat her.

The next morning everyone was moving more slowly because they had stayed up so very late. It wasn't hard for Qin to slip away from her older cousins. She was supposed to be gathering more sweet grass near the burrow opening, but nobody was paying much attention after the danger of the snake had been removed. It wasn't hard to find her way back to Snake's caved-in hole.

It didn't take very long for her to dig down. After all, she had learned how to dig tunnels when she was very small. The afternoon sun was slipping through the grass by the time she cleared away the last dirt. When the sunshine hit him he moved, just a little.

"Hello." He said. There was dirt on his tongue.

"Do you… do you eat prairie dogs?" Qin asked all in a rush.

"That's why we can't be friends." The amber eyes stared and his tongue flicked out nervously.

"But you wouldn't eat me would you, Snake?"

Tears welled in his eyes. "I will get hungry and I will want to eat you. That's what snakes do."

Qin thought about it. "Prairie dogs make families, that's what they do, but I don't always want to be around my family. And you don't want to live alone, like other snakes."

Snake looked at her and wiped a tear away with his rattle. "Then what will we do?" Snake's tongue flicked in and out.

"We'll keep being friends. You can eat bugs."

Snake tilted his head and looked at her. "What if I can't find enough bugs?"

"I'll catch them for you."

"What if bugs aren't enough?"

Qin crossed her arms. "Can you eat eggs? Sometimes there're eggs, on the prairie."

"I don't think I can eat eggs. Mice, or birds … sometimes lizards…"

"But not prairie dogs, right? Not prairie dogs."

Snake coiled around her. "I can try. I can go away to eat and come back. But what will we do when the others discover I'm not buried?"

"They just don't know you yet."

"I don't think they want to."

"This is going to be tricky." Qin stroked her whiskers while she thought and groomed Snake's head. "But don't worry. I'll teach you how to make friends."

Snake stared at Qin a long time. "I think you already have," he said. And he groomed Qin lightly between the ears.

Where's Margaret?

Helen Peppe

I lived on the dead-end section of a Maine country road for eighteen years. To live at the end of what someone had decided to label "dead," at an "end" that led to a cemetery full of dead people, didn't seem to me to be a good thing. The road had once been a throughway connecting towns, rich with vegetable stands and working farms. Those farms failed as farms often do, the people died, and the town terminated the road at the last house, our house, maintaining it as far as our mailbox only. The road deteriorated over the years to become what I knew it as: a narrow path of rocks, gravel, and exposed culverts, with seemingly endless woods to each side.

When night came, to the dead-end side, pitch black really meant black as pitch. City people, accustomed to street lamps and glowing house-lined streets, do not understand true darkness. I remember trying to explain "real" night to my fifth-grade classmates in Mr. Murphy's science class, and they just nodded. The teacher talked about how beautiful the stars must be, but I told him that you never considered looking up because you were too intent on trying to see what made the noises in front of you.

I thought the students understood until a few school friends visited me. Their first response when they held their hands in front of their faces without seeing them was, "Way cool," but when the coydogs (or dogotes) and coyotes began to yip and howl in the distance, and unseen things crashed through the woods, their second response, the one they held with them to tell the kids at school, was "I wouldn't want to live way out there. There's some crazy stuff happening in those woods."

Even inside, black encased the house, pushing at the windows. With the cemetery just up the road, my father decided our home was haunted by Margaret McKenney. He doesn't know himself what drew him to focus on Margaret. He says it might have been her name. Maybe he found some sadness in the fact that she died shortly after her children did. Maybe he was intrigued by the fact that Charles McKenney, her husband, married several times after she died and that those wives, too, were buried in the cemetery that also held the bones of a few Frazers—the only other name chiseled on the graves. Those slanting tombstones marked the resting spots of men and women who had worked the land that now grew wild on each side of the graveyard. The woods and fields hid old foundations, stone walls, and chimney fragments.

The grave markers, tilting backward and forward as the earth let go around them, tell a story about the men, women, and children who lived in the late 1700s to the late 1800s in the Auburn, Maine wilderness. Margaret McKenney died in 1834 at the age of 44, but her husband, Charles P. McKenney, lived more than a hundred years.

"It's just Margaret. She just wants to say hi," my father told us when the stairs groaned or the floors creaked, and no one appeared. "Hi there, Margaret," he would say to the air, a slight smile on his face. At the end of the day when we ate supper in the kitchen, and the wicker rocker chair rocked a bit forward then backward, he'd say, "Margaret gets tired, too," and although the rocker was his chair, the special one we could sit in only if he wasn't around, he sat somewhere else if he thought Margaret was in it. When a door slammed by itself, he would say (too seriously for my comfort) "Margaret's mad about something." Then he'd shake his head as if he were really confused, and say, "What'd one of you do now?"

Believing his every word, I narrowed my eyes and focused intently on the air. Sometimes I thought I saw something move just after I'd given up and I'd back away sharply, my heart filling my chest and ears with a deafening thumping at the prospect of meeting a ghost and possibly my death.

If anything was out of place, Margaret was responsible unless it was vegetables. Then the grumbling wild-haired man who lived in a rusty camper in the woods bordering our property was to blame.

Margaret was as much a member of our family as any of us, except she never got punished for causing trouble—a benefit of death. Nine children, one daughter's husband, and two grandkids stuffed into a five-bedroom house with short-tempered parents made me crave invisibility.

One of my older sisters, the reptile-loving one, was in trouble so often I thought she didn't want my mother to love her. She liked to walk up to the ledge behind the graveyard wall with my pretty sister, and drag me along as evidence of her innocence. My mother assumed I would tattle if she smoked or met a boy. She didn't know I refused to cross a sister who threw snakes at me and tickled me so hard I thought I would suffocate. Fear is stronger than loyalty. My sister told stories about Margaret to ensure my silence.

"There's blood matted in her long hair," she would tell me. "She hisses when she's mad. She's mad all the time because her eyes rotted away. She eats kids and leaves their bones for the coydogs because she hates stupid tattletales. She's gonna get you one of these nights."

I wouldn't go outside after dusk without my mother until I turned eleven and then I sprinted like the wind. I didn't know where Margaret was—in the barn knocking rakes over, in the house sitting transparently in the rocking chair, behind me in the black night that hid the world I stood in. Barefoot except in winter, I clung to my mother, not caring if she swatted my bottom or pinched my cheeks for my smart mouth. I tried to watch my mouth like she ordered, but it was difficult when all of my attention centered on survival.

"We shouldn't be out here by ourselves," I'd say. "You should do everything you're supposed to before it gets dark or wait until morning. What if Margaret has family with her? What if she doesn't like Daddy talking about her all the time? What if you can't protect me?"

"Don't you dare tell me what I should and shouldn't do or you'll be worrying about more than just a few ghosts," my mother snapped, annoyed at my pestering. "Don't be such a scaredy-cat."

We had barn cats, toms and unsprayed females prowling the farm, unvetted and unloved except by me and a few of my sisters. The cats wandered through the woods at night, slept in the spooky, shadowy barn, caught snakes and rats, and hid their kittens and themselves in frighteningly high places to escape my father and brothers who would drown them. The cats made me scream in surprise when they leapt out of the night to rub against my leg. Our barn cats were some of the bravest creatures I knew besides the sheep who were stupid. I was nothing like a cat.

*

My father composed his Margaret tales during supper. I was in bed with the light out shortly after he pushed away from the table. Fortunately, many of my siblings had aggression issues and dysfunctional communication skills, which made most suppers outright brawls and prevented any ghost stories from being told. Fear of the word "stupid" as a judgment on my intellect and flying objects kept my stomach jittery, but at least the fights allowed me to drop steak into the dog's mouth without getting caught.

Brother: "Who cooked this stupid steak? It's so tough I can't get my teeth through it."

Sister: "You know darn well who cooked the steak. Just shut your big fat mouth and eat it!"

Brother: "It's just like your stupid snickerdoodles, hard as rocks. I could use those cookies as hockey pucks, and they'd kill someone."

Sister: "You're a dirty fat liar. If you hate them so much, why do you eat them?"

Brother: "Worse than the slop I gave the pigs yesterday and that had maggots in it. Just like your ugly face."

A sister might then pick up a cup or a spoon, sometimes a potato, and throw it at the brother's head and shout, "You dumb stupid jerk. I hate you!"

The fights would end when my father slammed his fist on the table and bellowed, "Just shut up and eat the damn food!"

And my mother might either sit and cry quietly or shout about how we were all turning out bad no matter how hard she tried to make us good.

On summer nights when my oldest brother was home from Baptist Bible College, there might be half-chewed cobs of corn to throw.

He liked to tell us what he learned in college, explain God's plan for men and women. My mother stared hard at him over the bowls of boiled food and shouted, "Women are not meant to wait on men, you condescending pissant." She then threw her partially filled teacup at his head. He ducked and it hit the wall.

My father got up to inspect the damage: "Jesus, honey, did you have to dig the woodwork?"

But on calmer nights, when my father was in a good mood, he would sit back, lower his voice, and tell stories about Margaret, how she came down from the cemetery after climbing from her grave to haunt our house. I sat there, five years old, beside my mother, stomach tense, afraid to look behind me.

"A man died in the bedroom upstairs," my father told us. "In the room right above this kitchen." He pointed up to where my brother's room was. "He never woke up. Went to sleep and died. No one ever knew what happened. Something or someone killed him. Maybe it was Margaret, but maybe it was Mr. Cootsy. The bed is still up there."

Who was Mr. Cootsy? I went to bed that night with my head full of a second invisible person, wondering how many others I didn't yet know about.

Trembling beneath my blue bedspread, thinking how my parents had argued about what was true and what wasn't regarding the history of our house, my stomach churned with the certainty I wouldn't live through the night. Even with my nicest sister sleeping five feet across the room, I went to sleep with the covers pulled tight over my head, thinking anything exposed was fair game for ghosts and monsters.

"Don't let the bed bugs bite," my mother said before I finally got up the courage at age seven to explain that her words left me with the image of bugs where my feet would be, if I dared to stretch out my legs. After that she began to say, "Don't take any wooden nickels," which made me feel guilty because I'd recently stolen some of my father's butterscotch candies.

Then one night after she switched off the light...

Ooohhhh!!! A moan cut through the dark.

"What was that?" I screeched from beneath my blankets. I heard the thump of my sister's bed followed by a wail of terror that I can only liken to a rabbit's scream—viscerally frightening when you know rabbits as silent creatures.

I threw the covers off my head and sat up shouting, "Mamma! Mamma!" In the shadowy dark, I watched my sister's mattress and box spring begin to rise off the metal frame.

My mother burst in, ready to lay blame. "What's going on?"

That's when my father crawled out from under my nicest sister's bed, laughing.

"Stop trying to scare the girls," my mother shouted. "I have enough trouble as it is getting them to bed."

"Oh, they know I'm only joking around," my father defended himself. "They like to be scared. They're always watching that damned Scooby-Doo."

*

1975, I'm eight; ten years more before I can go down the road for good. My mean sister took me to the cemetery so she could sit on the ledge and smoke among the prickly juniper bushes. We crested the rocky hill and saw immediately that something was wrong. Margaret's tombstone stood as usual, but her grave was a big empty hole. A granite rectangular slab that must have rested above the coffin leaned against the far rock wall.

My sister stopped at the edge of the grave and looked down.

"Where's Margaret?" she said.

At the sound of her voice, a sudden rumbling and thundering of wings began as a flock of pheasants flew up from the stone wall. I screamed and ran as fast as I could.

"Ooohhh, the birds, they're gonna get you," my sister said, pretending to tremble in fear. She leaned against Margaret's tombstone and lit a cigarette.

The proof of the empty grave before me, I knew Margaret had escaped. As soon as I got home I told my mother. She didn't believe me and walked up the road to see for herself because we were, she oft repeated, all filthy liars.

She was surprised that I'd been right. When she saw the grave she didn't respond right away, just stared into the hole until she noticed the smell wafting off my older sister.

"That better not be cigarettes," she said looking around for a stick to whack her with. Then to me: "Either kids have been fooling around, or the town had reasons for digging her up."

I tried to accept her explanation, but I couldn't because kids robbing Margaret McKenney's grave was too much of a coincidence. There were lots of graves they could have chosen, like Henry Frazer's, which sat all by itself in the lower right corner of the cemetery. Why was our ghost's grave the only one that was empty?

I wonder now why my mother didn't call the town hall to inquire or report graveyard vandalism. I wonder why she didn't try to learn the truth. The grave remained empty for almost a year and then one day we walked up the road and it was filled again. My parents accepted the refilled grave just as they'd accepted the empty one, making up their own explanations and believing them—city maintenance, kids fooling around, or "sometimes these things just happen."

After Margaret's disappearance my father no longer talked about her haunting our house. Mr. Cootsy took the blame for creaks, groans, and things out of place. Without Margaret's physical remains, my father dismissed her completely. But I wasn't so sure.

One night—the rule being that none of us were supposed to get out of bed until after my mother had been up for half an hour or more—I had to pee so bad that I couldn't wait until morning. Heart beating in my ears, stomach trembling, I raced through the darkness down the stairs, turning on the light only when I got to the kitchen. Even the bright florescent did nothing to ease my something's-gonna-get-me instinct.

The house always felt alive, shifting and sighing as it settled. I looked briefly toward the wicker rocking chair in front of the window and, just as I did, it creaked. Terrified of what invisible thing was in it, I sprinted to the bathroom. When I finished and stepped into the dining room to get back to the kitchen hallway that led to the stairs, peripherally, I saw a shadow move on my left. I yelped, startled, and leapt backward against the wall next to the table. Fear really can paralyze a person. My legs refused to move forward but allowed my body to sink to the floor, my knees pressed against my chest. Then I heard a voice close to my ear.

"Shhhh," it said, dragging out the h's in a slow hiss of air.

There was nothing to do but scream for my mother to rescue me. Over and over, louder, higher, my throat raw.

She thumped down the stairs. "What?" Annoyance marked her syllables and she narrowed her far-sighted eyes at me, "What's all this ruckus over nothing?"

"Someone or something said shhhh," I answered, my stomach sick with stress.

"Well, do you blame them?" she asked, turning on the outside light and looking around. "You're making enough noise to raise the dead." Then after circling the four downstairs rooms, she said, "I don't see anyone and the dogs didn't bark. Go back to bed."

With my mother walking around and lights on, I felt brave enough to run upstairs.

The shhhh memory is as strong as my memory of Margaret's empty grave. If there are such things as ghosts or spirits, they would have known the importance of us kids being quiet at night. They would have heard the yelling and the punishments for getting out of bed, so I should have accepted the "shhhh" for the friendly warning it was. I question what it is about me that believed my mean sister when she claimed Margaret was out to get me. I always knew everything else she said was a lie.

A few weeks ago, I drove up the dead-end that led to my childhood home, to photograph Margaret's tombstone and those of her family. From a distance I could see my old house, no longer yellow but blue, sitting on the hill. Some other family lived there now, but it still looked ominous, haunted. Slowly I drove past the house that stared at me with its face-like windows, noticing how it still felt alive.

Blocked by a cable and boulders, I parked and walked up the narrow rock-covered hill. The sight of the graveyard surrounded by a low stone wall still sent a quiver of dread through my core, and I had to remind myself that the dread wasn't from anything real, but from made-up stories and years of teasing. Margaret McKenney's tombstone stood tipping a little back, just like always. She'd been accused of so much by my family, but in reality, she'd worked land, had a family, and died, probably hoping for the same things we all do: security and well-being.

Looking at her grave marker, I realized that I was her death age. When I was a child standing in the very same spot I'd thought forty-four years was old enough to die.

Had Margaret been the youngest child? A sister in a large family? Had she felt on edge as dusk approached, the pitch black dark pressing in on her? Had she heard coyotes and crashes through brush like I did at night, and had they filled her with an unease that left her nauseous with the driving need to get away?

The thing I wanted to know the most was where had she gotten to all those years ago when we found her grave empty? I'd called the town offices, searched the Internet for information on the McKenney cemetery, and asked the Historical Society, but there was no written record. Had she been bewildered by her poor luck of falling into a family she had nothing in common with beyond physical location, and decided to leave? Had she found a way out?

Margaret could have haunted our house, enjoying the stories, feeling a bit like a star after a back-sore life of planting, weeding, harvesting, and cleaning. Had she witnessed a scene between my parents or among the nine kids, a scene so horrible she couldn't bear to remain even as a spirit, and so left, taking her bones with her? Or was she simply dead, my father making up her ghost to explain what he didn't understand? Like the ancient people who created stories about gods and goddesses to make sense of their world?

I am the last in a line of nine, which as my mother can no longer make and carry new life, is in its way as dead an end as the last bit of road by our house or the life that ends in the grave. It doesn't really make a difference if Margaret McKenney was a ghost or just a story my father told. What matters is what I learned from her at eight years of age when we found that open grave: Even at a dead-end there is always hope of escape.

The Exiles, or Those Old English Vampires
Elsa Colón

They wake inside the walls at night and snarl,
and scent for something that can end their death,

for someone that can dry the tears of blood
that every night course down their cheeks of stone.

They wander through this brave new world,
not brave or new without a lord or goal,

just waiting for their daily grief at dawn—
that grief at dawn that only brings lament

and thoughts of heavens folding up like books,
too bright with words of love for beasts like them.

One might from loneliness remark some night
that you're his love, his light, his own—beware.

Blood Gothic

Nancy Holder

She wanted to have a vampire lover. She wanted it so badly that she kept waiting for it to happen. One night, soon, she would awaken to wings flapping against the window and then take to wearing velvet ribbons and cameo lockets around her delicate, pale neck. She knew it.

She immersed herself in the world of her vampire lover: She devoured Gothic romances, consumed late-night horror movies. Visions of satin capes and eyes of fire shielded her from the harshness of the daylight, from mortality and the vain and meaningless struggles of the world of the sun. Days as a kindergarten teacher and evenings with some overly eager, casual acquaintance could not pull her from her secret existence: always a ticking portion of her brain planned, proceeded, waited.

She spent her meager earnings on dark antiques and intricate clothes. Her wardrobe was crammed with white negligees and ruffled underthings. No crosses and no mirrors, particularly not in her bedroom. White tapered candles stood in pewter sconces, and she would read late into the night by their smoky flickerings, scented and ruffled, hair combed loosely about her shoulders. She glanced at the window often.

She resented lovers—though she took them, thrilling to the fullness of blood and life in them—who insisted upon staying all night, burning their breakfast toast and making bitter coffee. Her kitchen, of course, held nothing but fresh ingredients and copper and ironware; to her chagrin, she could not do without ovens or stoves of refrigerators. Alone, she carried candles and bathed in cool water.

She waited, prepared. And at long last, her vampire lover began to come to her in dreams. The two of them floated across the moors, glided through the fields of heather. He carried her to his crumbling castle, undressing her, pulling off her diaphanous gown, caressing her lovely body until, at the height of passion, he bit in her neck, drawing the life out of her and replacing it with eternal damnation and eternal love.

She awoke from these dreams drenched in sweat and feeling exhausted. The kindergarten children would find her unusually quite and self-absorbed, and it frightened them when she rubbed her spotless neck and smiled wistfully. *Soon and soon and soon*, her veins chanted, in prayer and anticipation. *Soon.*

The children were her only regret. She would not miss her inquisitive relatives and friends, the ones who frowned and studied her as if she were a portrait of someone they knew they were supposed to recognize; the ones who urged her to drop by for an hour, to come with them to films, to accompany them to the seashore; the ones who were connected to her—or thought they were—by the mere gesturing of the long and milky hands of Fate. Who sought to distract her from her one true passion; who sought to discover the secret of that passion. For, true to the sacredness of her vigil for her vampire lover, she had never spoken of him to a single earthbound soul. It would be beyond them, she knew. They would not comprehend a bond of such intentioned sacrifice.

But she would regret the children. Never would a child of their love coo and murmur in the darkness; never would his proud and noble features soften at the sigh of the mother and her child of his loins. It was her single sorrow.

Her vacation was coming. June hovered like the mist and the children squirmed in anticipation. Their own true lives would begin in June. She empathized with the shining eyes and smiling faces, knowing their wait was as agonizing as her own. Silently, as the days closed in, she bade each of them a tender farewell, holding them as they threw their little arms around her neck and pressed fervent summertime kisses on her cheeks.

She booked her passage to London on a ship. Then to Romania, Bulgaria, Transylvania. The hereditary seat of her beloved; the fierce, violent backdrop of her dreams. Her suitcases opened themselves to her long, full skirts and her brooches and lockets. She peered into her hand mirror as she packed it. "I am getting pale," she thought, and the idea both terrified and delighted her.

She became paler, thinner, more exhausted as her trip wore on. After recovering from the disappointment of the raucous, modern cruise ship, she raced across the Continent to find refuge in the creaky trains and taverns she had so yearned for. Her heart thrilled as she meandered past the black silhouettes of ruined fortresses and ancient manor houses. She sat for hours in the mists, praying for the howling wolf to find her, for the bat to come and join her.

She took to drinking wine in bed—deep, rich blood-red burgundy that glowed in the candlelight. She melted into the landscape within days, and cringed as if from the crucifix itself when flickers of her past life, her false American existence, invaded her serenity. She did not keep a diary; she did not count the days as her summer slipped away from her. She only rejoiced that she grew weaker.

It was when she was counting out the coins for a Gypsy shawl that she realized she had no time left. Tomorrow she must make for Frankfurt and from there fly back to New York. The shopkeeper nudged her, inquiring if she were ill, and she left with her treasure, trembling.

She flung herself on her rented bed. "This will not do. This will not do," she pleaded with the darkness. "You must come for me tonight. I have done everything for you, my beloved, loved you above all else. You must save me." She sobbed until she ached.

She skipped her last meal of veal and paprika and sat quietly in her room. The innkeeper brought her yet another bottle of burgundy and after she assured him that she was quite all right, just a little tired, he wished his guest a pleasant trip home.

The night wore on; though her book was open before her, her eyes were riveted to the windows, her hands clenched around the wine glass as she sipped steadily, like a creature feeding. Oh, to feel him against her veins, emptying her and filling her!

Soon, soon, soon...

Then all at once, it happened. The windows rattled, flapped inward. A great shadow, a curtain of ebony, fell across the bed, and the room began to whirl, faster, faster still; and she was consumed with a bitter, deathly chill. She heard, rather than saw, the wine glass crash to the floor, and struggled to keep her eyes open as she was overwhelmed, engulfed, taken.

"Is it you?" she managed to whisper through teeth that rattled with delight and cold and terror. "Is it finally to be?"

Freezing hands touched her everywhere: her face, her breasts, the desperate offering of her arched neck. Frozen and strong and never-dying. Sinking, she smiled in a rictus of mortal dread and exultation. Eternal damnation, eternal love. Her vampire lover had come for her at last.

When her eyes opened again, she let out a howl and shrank against the searing brilliance of the sun. Hastily, they closed the curtains and quickly told her where she was: home again, where everything was warm and pleasant and she was safe from the disease that had nearly killed her.

She had been ill before she had left the States. By the time she had reached Transylvania, her anemia had been acute. Had she never noticed her own pallor, her lassitude?

Anemia. Her smile was a secret on her white lips. So they thought, but he *had* come for her, again and again. In her dreams. And on that night, he had meant to take her to his castle forever, to crown her the best-beloved one, his love of the moors and the mists.

She had but to wait, and he would finish the deed.

Soon, soon, soon.

She let them fret over her, wrapping her in blankets in the last days of summer. She endured the forced cheer of her relatives, allowed them to feed her rich food and drink in hopes of restoring her.

But her stomach could no longer hold the nourishment of their kind; they wrung their hands and talked of stronger measures when it became clear that she was wasting away.

At the urging of the doctor, she took walks. Small ones at first, on painfully thin feet. Swathed in wool, cowering behind sunglasses, she took tiny steps like an old woman. As she moved through the summer hours, her neck burned with an ungovernable pain that would not cease until she rested in the shadows. Her stomach lurched at the sight of grocery-store windows. But at the butcher's, she paused, and licked her lips at the sight of the raw, bloody meat.

But she did not go in. She grew neither worse nor better.

"I am trapped," she whispered to the night as she stared into the flames of a candle by her bed. "I am disappearing between your world and mine, my beloved. Help me. Come for me." She rubbed her neck, which ached and throbbed but showed no outward signs of his devotion. Her throat was parched, bone-dry, but water did not quench her thirst.

At long last, she dreamed again. Her vampire lover came for her as before, joyous in their reunion. They soared above the crooked trees at the foothills, steamed like black banners above the mountain crags to his castle. He could not touch her enough, workshop her enough and they were wild in their abandon as he carried her in her diaphanous gown to the gates. Of his fortress.

But at the entrance, he shook his head with sorrow and could not let her pass into the black realm with him. His fiery tears seared her neck, and she thrilled to the touch of the mark even as she cried out for him as he left her, fading into the vapors with a look of entreaty in his dark, flashing eyes.

Something was missing; he required a boon of her before he could bind her against his heart. A thing that she must give to him...

She walked in the sunlight, enfeebled, cowering. She thirsted, hungered, yearned. Still she dreamed of him, and still he could not take the last of her into himself.

Days and nights and days. Her steps took her finally to the schoolyard, where once, only months before, she had embraced and kissed the children, thinking never to see them again. They were all there, who had kissed her cheeks so eagerly. Their silvery laughter was like the tinkling of bells as dust motes from their games whirled around their feet. How free they seemed to her who was so troubled, how content and at peace.

The children.

She shambled forward, eyes widening behind the shields of smoky glass.

He required something of her first.

Her one regret. Her only sorrow.

She thirsted. The burns on her neck pulsated with pain.

Tears of gratitude welled in her eyes for the revelation that had not come too late. Weeping, she pushed open the gate of the schoolyard and reached out a skeleton-limb to a child standing apart from the rest, engrossed in a solitary game of cat's cradle. Tawny-headed, ruddy-cheeked, filled with the blood and the life.

For him, as a token of their love.

"My little one, do you remember me?" she said softly.

The boy turned. And smiled back uncertainly in innocence and trust.

Then, as she came for him, swooped down on him like a great, winged thing, with eyes that burned through the glasses, teeth that flashed once, twice…

Soon, soon, soon.

Contributor Biographies

Karen Bovenmyer loves working for Iowa State University's Center for Excellence in Learning and Teaching where she helps graduate students prepare for college teaching. A native Iowan, she holds a BS in anthropology, English, and history and an MA in creative writing and literature. She is currently earning her MFA in creative writing (Popular Fiction) through Stonecoast, University of Southern Maine. She dedicates this story to her parents, who taught her to love all critters great and small, and would like to extend special thanks to Christiana Langenberg and @gradfiction554.

Elsa Colón was born and raised in San Juan, Puerto Rico. Elsa currently lives in Denver, Colorado, where she works at the Denver Public Library. She studied English, Spanish, and French at the University of Denver, and she just received her MFA from Stonecoast with a Poetry concentration.

Libby Cudmore's stories and essays have appeared in recent issues of *Needle, Mysterical-E, The MacGuffin, The Yalobusha Review, The Chaffey Review, The Southern Women's Review, Sunsets and Silencers, Red Fez, Inertia, Xenith,* and *Big Pulp* (with Matthew Quinn Martin). She is an editor at *The Midnight Diner* and a frequent contributor to *Battered Suitcase, Shaking Like a Mountain, Celebrities in Disgrace, Crime Factory, Hardboiled, A Twist of Noir,* and *Thrillers, Killers 'n' Chillers,* where her story "Unplanned" won a Bullet award in 2009 and was a finalist for the 2010 Derringer award in flash fiction.

Poet and lawyer **Jessica de Koninck's** collection *Repairs* is published by Finishing Line Press. Her poems appear in a wide variety of journals and anthologies, including *The Paterson Literary Review, The Ledge,* and *U.S. 1 Worksheets.* A longtime resident of Montclair, New Jersey, she holds an M.F.A. from Stonecoast. For more, please visit www.jessicadekoninck.com.

Julia Gay was born and raised in Baton Rouge, Louisiana. She received her BA from the College of Santa Fe. She graduated from Stonecoast in the summer of 2011 with an MFA in Poetry. She has read her work on episode 20 of *Zinecore Radio*, which can be found at www.blogtalkradio.com/thezineshow. She writes and lives in New Mexico. Her website is www.jgaywriting.com.

Nancy Holder is a multiple Bram Stoker Award winner as well as a *New York Times* bestselling author (the *Wicked* series), who, with her coauthor, Debbie Viguié, has sold two more young adult series, *Crusade* and *Wolf Springs Chronicles*. She and Erin Underwood write a column together for the *Science Fiction Writers of America Bulletin*. She lives in San Diego with her daughter, Belle, two corgis, and three cats. Visit her at www.nancyholder.com, on Facebook, and on Twitter.

Jeff Kass teaches Creative Writing at Pioneer High School in Ann Arbor, Michigan, and at Eastern Michigan University in Ypsilanti, Michigan, and also serves as the Programming Director for the Ann Arbor Book Festival and the Literary Arts Director at Ann Arbor's Teen Center—The Neutral Zone. *Invisible Staircase*, a chapbook of poems, was published by Winged City Press in January 2010. His one-man performance poetry show *Wrestle the Great Fear* debuted in April 2009, and a collection of essays and poems from his blog "From the Front of the Room" won first place in the 2010 Teacher's Voice chapbook contest. A teaching guidebook *Underneath: The Archaeological Approach to Teaching Creative Writing*, co-authored with Scott Beal, debuted from Red Beard Press in June 2001 and Jeff's short story collection *Knuckleheads* was released from Dzanc Books in April 2011.

James Patrick Kelly has written novels, short stories, essays, reviews, poetry, plays, and planetarium shows. His short novel *Burn* won the Science Fiction Writers of America's Nebula Award in 2007. He has won the World Science Fiction Society's Hugo Award twice: in 1996, for his novelette "Think Like A Dinosaur," and in 2000, for his novelette "Ten to the Sixteenth to One." His fiction has been translated into eighteen languages. With John Kessel he is co-editor of *Feeling Very Strange: The Slipstream Anthology*. He is on the faculty of the Stonecoast Creative Writing MFA Program. His website is www.jimkelly.net.

Michael Kimball is a novelist, playwright, and screenwriter. His novel *Undone* received the Fresh Talent Award in the U.K. and remained on the *London Times'* top ten bestseller list for two months in 1996. Stage plays include *Ghosts of Ocean House*, nominated for the 2007 Edgar Award by the Mystery Writers of America, and the award-winning short play *Say No More*, which has seen multiple performances by more than 25 companies across the country. Michael has sold original screenplays and adaptations to movie companies and written episodes for the TV series Monsters.

Paul Kirsch is the product of *Twilight Zone* marathons and old-timey radio dramas. He earned his BA in "Fantasy Writing & Sub-Creation through Cultural Storytelling" from the Johnston Center at the University of Redlands in 2007. He earned his MFA in creative writing with an emphasis in Popular Fiction from the Stonecoast program at the University of Southern Maine in 2011. Find out more about Paul, his works, and what he's reading at www.paul-kirsch.com.

A.J. Luxton firmly believes you can mix science and myth and not wake up with a terrible hangover. AJ, who swears by a constant regimen of coffee, cat hair and higher education, graduated from the Stonecoast MFA program in 2007 and writes in the gorgeous city of Portland, Oregon. Find AJ's fiction in *Eldritch Skies*, a tabletop role-playing game of Lovecraftian SF, and visit the *Science Monologues Project* and *Strange As Truth* blog at www.ajluxton.com.

Julie L. Martin (formerly Julie Scharf) is a lover and writer of creative nonfiction and has published several short stories, essays, and poems. She is the author of short creative nonfiction pieces titled "The Train of Bobby's Life," "Remnants," and "Signals." Born and raised in the suburbs of Chicago, Illinois, she now resides in Colorado.

Matthew Quinn Martin is a graduate of the Stonecoast MFA Program, University of Southern Maine. He is also the writer of the crime drama *Slingshot*, a feature film starring Julianna Margulies, David Arquette, Thora Birch, Balthazar Getty, and

Joely Fisher, available on DVD from the Weinstein Co. Visit him at www.matthewquinnmartin.com.

J.M. McDermott is the author of five novels, including *Never Knew Another*, *Maze*, and *Last Dragon*. He has a BA in creative writing from the University of Houston, and an MFA from the University of Southern Maine's Stonecoast Program. He lives east of Atlanta, in a maze of bookshelves, empty coffee cups, and crazy schemes.

Sandra McDonald's recent story collection *Diana Comet and Other Improbable Stories* won a Lambda Literary Award for transgender fiction. It is also a 2010 Booklist Editor's Choice and an American Library Association "Over the Rainbow" book. She is also the author of three science fiction novels and two upcoming young adult mysteries for gay and straight teens. Her work has appeared in more than forty magazines and anthologies. Visit her at www.sandramcdonald.com.

Ellen Neuborne is a writer, editor and ghostwriter living in New York City. She holds a BA in classics from Brown University and an MFA in Popular Fiction from the University of Southern Maine/Stonecoast. Her fiction has appeared in *Thuglit*, *The Chick Lit Review*, and *Cellstories*. She's at work on a short story collection titled *Mommy Noire*.

Helen Peppe's writings and photographs have appeared in magazines, including *Practical Horseman*, *Dog Fancy*, *Mused Literary Review*, and *Cats Magazine*. She is the author of the limited edition *Live on Stage: A History of the State Theater*. Two stories from her memoir *Pigs Can't Swim* will appear in upcoming anthologies *PaniK* and *Telling Our Stories*. Helen's writing has placed first in the Richard Carbonneau Fiction Contest, the WordWorth 2009 Essay and Fiction Contest, The Starving Writer Literary contest, May and August 2010. Helen was a finalist for the 2011 Annie Dillard Creative Nonfiction Award and the 2011 Maine Literary Awards.

Michaela Roessner has published four novels, and shorter works in venues including *Asimov's Magazine*, *F&SF*, *OMNI Magazine*, *Room Magazine*, and assorted anthologies. Her novel *Walkabout*

Woman won the Crawford and John W. Campbell awards. She's had pieces short-listed for the Calvino Prize, the Tiptree Award, and the Millennium Publishing contest. Recent publications include "Crumbs," published in *F&SF* in 2010, and "The Fishes Speak," in P.S. Publishing's fall 2010 anthology. Her bestiary chapter "The Klepsydra" is available in the 2011 autumn issue of *F&SF*. She teaches creative writing at Western State College of Colorado's low-residency MFA program, and online classes for Gotham Writers' Workshop.

Linda K. Sienkiewicz is a writer and artist. Her poetry has been published in *Prairie Schooner, Clackamas Literary Review, Rattle, Permafrost, Controlled Burn, Driftwood Review, Spoon River Poetry Review, Main Street Rag,* and others, and her short stories have appeared in the Cleis Press anthology *Frenzy, A Twist of Noir,* and other online and print literary journals. Her artwork has been featured in *Calyx, From East to West: Bicoastal Verse, Tar Wolf Review,* and *The MacGuffin.* Among her awards is a 1997 poetry chapbook award from Heartland and a Pushcart Prize Nomination. She has an MFA from Stonecoast.

Patricia Smith's books include *Blood Dazzler,* a finalist for the 2008 National Book Award, and one of NPR's top five books of 2008; and *Teahouse of the Almighty,* a National Poetry Series selection. Her work has appeared or is forthcoming in *Poetry, The Paris Review, TriQuarterly,* and *Best American Poetry 2011* and *Best American Essays 2011.* She is a professor at the College of Staten Island, and teaches for Cave Canem and in the Stonecoast MFA program.

Scott Wolven is the author of *Controlled Burn* (Scribner). Wolven's stories have appeared seven years in a row in *The Best American Mystery Stories* series (Houghton Mifflin), the most consecutive appearances in the history of the series. The title story from *Controlled Burn* appeared in *The Best American Noir of the Century* (Houghton Mifflin), edited by James Ellroy and Otto Penzler. Wolven's work was featured in Vintage America, with pictures by Patricia de Gorostarzu and Foreword by Kyle Eastwood, Clint Eastwood's son, for the 2010 Festival America in Vincennes, France. He was called a Future Master of Noir in Library Journal. Wolven's novels *False Hopes* and *King Zero* are forthcoming in 2012 from Grove/The Mysterious Press. He is finishing another collection of short stories and is working on projects with Noir Nation. Wolven is on the faculty of the Stonecoast MFA Program, University of Southern Maine.

About the Editors

Hannah Strom-Martin's fiction has appeared in *Realms of Fantasy Magazine, OnSpec, Andromeda Spaceways Inflight Magazine,* and the anthology *Amazons: Sexy Tales of Strong Women.* Her nonfiction has appeared in *The North Bay Bohemian, The Sacramento News and Review, North Bay Biz Magazine,* and *Fantasy Magazine,* for whom she recently interviewed author Jacqueline Carey. For the last five years she has been a contributing literary critic for *Strange Horizons Online.* She is a graduate of Bennington College (BA), the University of Southern Maine's Stonecoast MFA Program, and the Odyssey Fantasy Writers' Workshop. She currently resides in California.

Erin Underwood coauthors a column for the *SFWA Bulletin,* she was the co-editor of March Interstitial Madness for the Interstitial Arts Foundation's blog in 2011, and she is also the founder of the Book Bloggers Association and the popular fiction literary blog Underwords. Erin has a degree in creative writing and literature from the Harvard University Extension School and earned her MFA in Creative Writing from the University of Southern Maine's Stonecoast MFA program. She is a fiction writer, interviewer, reviewer, blogger, and assistant for hire. She lives in Marblehead, Massachusetts with her husband. Her website is www.underwordsblog.com.

Copyright Acknowledgments

.

Made in the USA
Lexington, KY
08 December 2011